First Flight Feathers

The Best of Worship Live

— EDITED BY —

GILLIAN WARSON & JANET WOOTTON

Sacristy Press

Sacristy Press
PO Box 612, Durham, DH1 9HT

www.sacristy.co.uk

First published in 2023 by Sacristy Press, Durham

Copyright © Gillian Warson & Janet Wootton 2023
The moral rights of the editors have been asserted.

All rights reserved, no part of this publication may be reproduced or transmitted in any form or by any means, electronic, mechanical photocopying, documentary, film or in any other format without prior written permission of the publisher.

Scripture quotations, unless otherwise stated, are from the New Revised Standard Version Bible: Anglicized Edition, copyright © 1989, 1995 National Council of the Churches of Christ in the United States of America. Used by permission. All rights reserved worldwide.

Every reasonable effort has been made to trace the copyright holders of material reproduced in this book, but if any have been inadvertently overlooked the publisher would be glad to hear from them.

Sacristy Limited, registered in England & Wales, number 7565667

British Library Cataloguing-in-Publication Data
A catalogue record for the book is available from the British Library

ISBN 978-1-78959-285-6

The Editors would like to thank the Pratt Green Trust and The Hymn Society for funding towards this publication.

A website accompanying this book can be found via
www.sacristy.co.uk/book/worship-live
where you can find more information about authors and composers, and get involved in the conversation.

Contents

Preface viii

1. All things good and medical. 1
2. And I have called you by name 3
3. And the elder brother 4
4. Article 5
5. Away in a manger we choose to find Christ 8
6. Bless the Lord all created things 9
7. Bright Sunday's waving palms are fading fast. 11
8. By a monument of marble 12
9. By grace bestowed, so undeserved 14
10. By the light of a flickering lantern. 16
11. Caedmon 18
12. Can you trace the pattern of the rays of the sun? 20
13. Choosing to return home. 22
14. Clap your hands all you trees!. 24
15. Colliding with God 26
16. Come dare to live in the world today. 27
17. Come, for everything's ready. 28
18. Come in to the warmth. 30
19. Come, vast eternal dance of one-in-three. 32
20. Crying for the world 34
21. Deep in the core of earth 36
22. Deep in the heart of God 38
23. Don't forget your lunch box. 40
24. Early Easter morning—all were sunk in fear 42
25. Founder of the laws of motion 44

26. Gentle to understand... 46
27. Go canny Brother Aidan! Iona's rocks are sharp................ 47
28. God became a man in Jesus..................................... 49
29. God of love and grace... 51
30. God of my faith, I offer you my doubt......................... 52
31. God of the galaxies spinning in space......................... 54
32. Great is God's truth, it shall prevail........................ 56
33. Held captive by the king of love.............................. 57
34. Holy Spirit hovering, brooding................................ 58
35. Hopkins, your bright kestrel.................................. 60
36. How are we to sing our songs to you?.......................... 62
37. How did it come to this?...................................... 65
38. I believe in God, Creator, Image maker........................ 67
39. I wish that my eyes were fountains of tears................... 69
40. I wonder, might Joseph.. 70
41. I wouldn't touch him with a bargepole......................... 72
42. Imagine a world where our leaders aren't liars................ 74
43. In a land that was parched and baked dry by sun............... 76
44. In affairs of economics....................................... 79
45. In the dark before the dawn................................... 81
46. In the silence of the midnight................................ 83
47. In the stillness of this moment............................... 86
48. Journeying on a day of darkness............................... 88
49. Knowing us from eternity...................................... 90
50. Lady in the Shadows... 92
51. Let justice roll like waters.................................. 94
52. Lift me up on your shoulder, Shepherd......................... 96
53. Listen! Mary tells the story.................................. 99
54. Lord God, we thank you....................................... 101
55. Lord Jesus, help us stand.................................... 103
56. Love soars where eagles cease to fly......................... 104
57. Millions of migrants, on the run............................. 107
58. Must we starve our children to pay our debts?................ 108
59. My God is beyond all imagining............................... 110
60. My mother—she was lovely!.................................... 112

61. No height so high, no depth so low 114
62. O God, by whom our yesterdays............................. 116
63. Oh my Spirit will flow like the river of life 118
64. O sun of Wisdom, arise...................................... 120
65. Oh the bliss of a bit of shelter 122
66. On Calvary, life's light 124
67. Our wonder grows and deepens with the years 126
68. Present at the world's creation............................... 128
69. Ruth, don't do it 130
70. See he comes in modest manner............................. 132
71. She threw the bucket down the well 134
72. Sing praise for Hebrew midwives............................. 135
73. Soaked by the spray from these turbulent waters 137
74. The holiness of God is veiled................................. 139
75. The soldiers by and large were decent men 141
76. These are the hands... 144
77. To pray is to extol 146
78. Tread softly 148
79. Tree of wisdom, give us shelter 150
80. We celebrate God's word to us............................... 152
81. We happily could spend our days............................ 154
82. We know the songs of Zion from our youth................... 155
83. WE LOVE 158
84. Weep with us for the islands 161
85. When mountains that we thought secure..................... 163
86. When seen from vastnesses of space 164
87. When the body's racked with pain........................... 166
88. When the church of Jesus.................................... 168
89. Who knows now?.. 170
90. Why stand gazing?.. 171
91. Worlds of wonders teeming round us 172

Conclusion.. 175
Bibliography.. 177
Copyright Acknowledgments 180

Index of Composers 185
Index of Tunes 187
Index of Authors 189
Index of First lines and titles 191
Index of Bible texts 194

Preface

Gillian Warson and I are delighted to be able to introduce to you this collection of the "Best of Worship Live", under the title: *First Flight Feathers*. The title is taken from one of the poems in the book, "Landfall with Columba", by Maggie Norton, which celebrates the craft of beautiful writing—you need to read the poem to see the context.

The first flight feathers of a swan are ideally suited to creating a perfect manuscript, conveying the word of God to a new generation. For the present book, the phrase has a double meaning. *Worship Live* has certainly honoured and nourished the many crafts involved in writing effective resources for worship, honing skills and sharpening tools, as we have worked with worship makers over the years. But we have also, to our great delight, given *first flight* to many who emerged newly fledged, feeling the wind of the Spirit under their wings, but tentative in trusting to their new plumage.

We have been able to do this because of the generous support of many established writers, composers, poets and worship makers over the years. We were in business long enough (about 20 years) for some of our new writers to establish their reputations, and, in turn, reach out to others by offering online editorial advice, or contributing to the writing weekends that became such a feature of the *Worship Live* community.

The publication grew out of an idea by the amazing hymnological entrepreneur Bernard Braley of Stainer & Bell, who had been at the forefront of publishing new words and music for worship for a generation and more. I had just finished working with June Boyce-Tillman on a hymn resource for the WCC Decade for the Churches in Solidarity with Women, *Reflecting Praise* (1993), under his guidance, and he approached me with a view to embarking on a new worship journal, initially titled *Living Liturgy*. I, of course, leapt at the opportunity to work with Bernard Braley and Stainer & Bell. We gathered a small group to work on the idea, and *Worship Live* was launched at St Martin-in-the-Fields on 18 June 1995.

Stainer & Bell helped to develop and continued to publish the journal for 17 years. We built up a wonderful working relationship with the staff there, who have continued to be supportive in preparation of the present book.

We met first at Union Chapel, Islington (now a major Arts and Community venue), where I was minister at the time. Gradually more people joined the editorial team, and for a while we split into three groups, meeting in the South, North and West of Britain, each taking responsibility for one of the three issues a year. There was a steady flow of wonderful material, which I collected into lever-arch files, and carted in an enormous suitcase by train all over the country to whichever venue was hosting the committee meeting.

At the meetings, we fell on the mass of material like starving people at a feast, and worked with great intensity to distil the 30 or so items that would create the next issue, and guide our thinking for the next year. Trusting in God's Spirit, we allowed new themes to emerge, to be listed on the back page of each issue, to give people several months to work on them. This meant that the themes were very varied, including Prayer and Spirituality; Starting (or Ending) points for worship; The Trinity (four issues—I know!); Justice and Prophecy; War and Peace; the Created World and many more.

Because the themes emerged from, as well as shaping, the flow of material, there was room for ideas to develop. For example, there was often, naturally enough, a strong biblical focus. This led to occasional specifically biblical themes, such as the wilderness, or prophecy, or storytelling in scripture and beyond. These, in turn, brought out new insights into well-known biblical passages, such as two in these pages looking at the parable of the Prodigal Son from different perspectives.

We heard from biblical characters who were often hidden under layers of narrative. Often these are women, such as the Hebrew midwives, Job's wife, or Peter's mother-in-law. However, not all "bit parts" are female, as, for example David and Bathsheba's *first* son, who died in infancy.

The figure of Divine Wisdom opens to us the opportunity to address femaleness in relation to God, and several writers explore the creative significance of the image of God as fully present in women as well as men.

Each issue also contained a section on a season of the Church year, and other relevant seasonal events. This meant that we produced a regular output of new material on Advent, Christmas, the Easter season and so on, and marked a whole host of events such as One World Week, Homelessness Sunday and Education Sunday.

We were publishing during interesting and often difficult times, and because of our reasonably rapid turnover, we could bring responses to the conflict in Bosnia, or the Dunblane massacre, or 9/11, or the London bombings, soon enough after the event for them to be useful. Our writers were often deeply involved in global networks, so that we included material written and used in relation to Hong Kong in 1997, the Drop the Debt Campaign and the 1998 G8 summit, and the 2007 commemoration of the ending of the transatlantic trade in enslaved people from Africa to the Americas, the root of so much devastating inequality in our own time.

Worship Live began, as already mentioned, during the WCC Decade for the Churches in Solidarity with Women, and one of the early issues included hymns and poems from the mid-Decade Conference held in Durham, at which an icon of St Hilda was commissioned, and installed at Durham Cathedral. Her story, with many others, was part of a celebration of individuals who contributed to our shared heritage.

Not all the themes were successful. In 2012, we attempted to focus on the "other side" of the Restoration of 1662—the Great Ejectment of non-conformist clergy, and the development of Dissent, political and religious, as a powerful element in the narrative of Britain. Not a single item came in on the theme! So we wryly acknowledged the fact, and based the issue in question on something else.

Our writers drew on their own vivid experiences of Christian life, not all benign. Some wrote from their experience as Survivors of abuse, including sexual abuse in the Church. Many wrote of the difficulty of discipleship, of their doubts as well as their faith, of their struggles with physical impairment or mental anguish, frailty and fear. And of course there was room for laughter, explosions of joy, appreciation of human love and the glorious beauty of life as well.

We grappled with the language of faith in a world that is very different from the pre-scientific era in which our hymns and liturgies have their roots, recognizing from the very first item in the book, that healing involves medical care as well as miracles, scientific advance alongside prayer. And the human race cannot afford to retreat from engagement with developments in cosmology, ecology or genetic research, but must take responsibility before God, for the ways in which we pursue and use new knowledge.

This topic formed the focus of one of our writers' weekends towards the end of the publication of *Worship Live*. These weekends were held for over a decade, organized first by Mike and Carolyn Sanderson, then Marlene Phillips, and afterwards Gillian Warson. They were extremely productive. Typically, we would gather to hear members of the editorial team speaking about the theme of the weekend, and about the skills of writing words and music. The participants would spend a day writing, and then gather in the evening, rather nervously, to display the results of their efforts before the assembled company for comments. On the Sunday morning, we would share communion, using the hymns and tunes we had written over the weekend, sometimes a dozen or more. The end was always joyful, as we astonished ourselves with the creativity of the process, and praised God.

So strong was the network built up at the writing weekends that they continued to flourish for some years after *Worship Live* ceased publication, only running into the ground, as so much else has done, in the pandemic. But even then, the residue of funds that had been built up has been offered for writing workshops at *Hymn Society* Conferences, where a number of the participants are also active members.

The writers' weekends were symptomatic of something that grew into a fundamental characteristic of *Worship Live*: that it was as much a community as a publication. This started from the very first issue, in which we invited composers to submit new tunes to the hymn texts. The second issue included a tune by Marlene Phillips to a text by Bernard Braley, published in the first, and so it went on. Some texts attracted two or three or more tunes, which demonstrated how composers responded to the nuances of hymn words.

Over time, partnerships emerged, which, as Hazel Hudson's article describes, went out into the wider world through hymn competitions and publications in books and online. This was an absolute delight to see. Hazel Hudson's article was written for a special celebratory issue, no. 50, in which we invited contributors to tell their stories. So many spoke of the influence of *Worship Live* and how much they valued both the publication and the network.

You will recognize in these pages the names of prominent writers, but you will also find many who were writing for the first time. You will see the links with writing weekends, and partnerships between writers and composers as they developed. Above all, we hope you will find poems, hymns, songs and stories that lift your heart and challenge your mind, and bring you close to God.

Now, turn the page, and join the feast.

Janet Wootton
January 2023

1. All things good and medical

7.6.7.6 & refrain   Suggested tune: ALL THINGS BRIGHT AND BEAUTIFUL

All things good and medical,
all research great and small,
all things new and technical,
you are the Lord of all.

1. The scanner and the x-ray,
the E.C.G. machines,
the pacemaker and battery,
and new research on genes.
Chorus

2. New hips and knees and elbows,
replacement and repair,
corneal and kidney transplants
are given by those who care.
Chorus

3. The laser and the surgeon
bring eyesight to the blind.
New implants bring new hearing
and wholeness to the mind.
Chorus

4. For all these things we thank you
for you are Lord of NOW.
There's nothing been invented
without you knowing how.
Chorus

Sue Wade and members of Latimer Congregational
Church, Stepney (Thursday Fellowship)

Sue Wade, Minister of Latimer Church, Stepney, commented:

> The Thursday fellowship meeting at Latimer Chapel is a small fellowship of local ladies whose ages range from 60–100 years.
>
> At one of these meetings, we looked at issues which concerned us as individuals. We looked at our personal prayer life, and we discovered that we are always ready to take our aches and pains, our disabilities and our health to the Lord, but did not often readily acknowledge that he is already involved with the treatments that we receive to enhance our quality of life.
>
> Everyone contributed to a list of some of the things experienced by the group and the treatments they had received, and I put them together so that whenever we sing this hymn, we will be reminded that even technology is from God and that, in this, we should take comfort and give him thanks. We used this hymn at our Sunday evening worship in which some of the group members took part on the theme of Prayer and Praise.

2. And I have called you by name

Nicholas Danks

Music © Copyright 2007 Stainer & Bell Ltd. Reprinted by permission.

And I have called you by name,
called you by name,
called you by name
and you are mine.
(Isaiah 43:1b)

Prayer response by Nicholas Danks, then Director of Music at St Martin-in-the-Fields, Trafalgar Square, London.

The issue editor comments:

> Each year, a service in memory of those who have died street homeless is held at St Martin-in-the-Fields. The service is prepared by members of the St Martin's clergy, the Social Care Unit, and *UNLEASH* (London Churches Homelessness co-ordination). Last year (2002), the service followed a simple repeating pattern. At its heart was the reading of the names of those who had died, in four sections, each followed by a time of silence and prayers. A Tibetan Prayer Bell was used to mark the beginning and end of the silences. The prayers are by Janet Wootton, then chair of *UNLEASH*.

The full text with prayers can be found in *Eagles' Wings* (2007, pp. 118–21).

3. And the elder brother

Conversion
And the elder brother
wasted his substance
in joyless living, hoarding
his share of the inheritance
and living in plenty
while the years passed.

Then he came to himself and said,
"I have enough and to spare,
and have no need that any
should give to me. I will arise
and go to my father and say:
'Father, I have sinned against heaven
and in your sight. I have lived
like one of your hired servants.
I will take my share of the inheritance,
and seek for those like my brother
who have no-one to give to them,
who know only starvation and loss
of friends and of dignity.'
And to them I will say,
'Let us return to our father together,
for he will welcome us both
when he sees his family restored,
and our arms around each other.'"

Alan Horner
First published in the *Epworth Review*.

Worship Live often included different perspectives on Bible passages. This account of the story often known as "The Prodigal Son" is told from the point of view of the elder brother. Another, at no. 13, explores the younger son's relationship with their father.

4. Article

My subscription to *Worship Live* began in 2004, after Stainer & Bell sent me a complimentary copy. However, I then never realized where this would lead, or the opportunity for professional fulfilment which it was to offer, especially after a stroke prevented me playing organ or piano.

Several of the authors whose texts I set have given me the opportunity to invent more music. Among them are Peter Millam, Joan Heybourn, Pam Gidney, John Coutts and a Scottish-born lady resident in America, named Edith Sinclair Downing, in whose book, *For Us, God's People Now* (2011), two of my hymn settings are to appear. Then there is Donald Burling, who is compiling a collection called *Sermons in Song* (see <https://sermonsinsong.wordpress.com/>), for which I have provided a number of harmonizations together with a few tunes, sometimes with a third person involved. Indeed, from time to time, my work with him has spawned collaborations with other authors. But none of my lyricists has been as prolific as Hugh G. Wetmore, a Baptist minister resident in South Africa, and the author of *Singing the Word* (see <https://gatewaynews.co.za/singing-the-word-to-one-another-hugh-wetmore/>), an ongoing set of texts, to over a hundred of which I have either supplied the harmonies or the complete score, in each case also writing a simpler version with guitar accompaniment.

In 2009 and 2010, entries to the UK Song Writing Contest (<https://www.songwritingcontest.co.uk/>), eleven in all, have produced the following combined results—one Finalist (text: Peter Millam), and eight Semi-Finalists (with texts by Hugh Naunton, Hugh G. Wetmore and myself), plus one by myself and Donald Burling, who also wrote the tune, which I harmonized.

Recently I have had ten settings for three-part choir (sopranos, altos and men) entitled *Welcome, child of Mary*, accepted by animus Music Publishing. Of these works, four began as a direct result of words published in *Worship Live* (asterisked) and two through connection, via this magazine, with the authors, namely:

1. Peter Millam ("Mary's Obedience"* and "A Festive-time Calypso")

2. Pam Gidney ("Come Messiah"* and "The Far and Near Calypso"*)
3. John Lansley ("Sleeping Joseph"*)
4. Hugh Wetmore, whose verses and tune, "Come Home for Christmas", I have arranged.

A fruitful and ecumenical output!

I was also much encouraged by the perceptive and challenging Guest Editorial by Andrew Pratt (*Worship Live* no. 47) as, for a long time, I have felt it necessary not only to de-mythologize but also to reinterpret the Creed on my own terms. When reading Church history, I tend to empathize with the "heretics" and to feel, at least, that they had a point.

As Leslie Weatherhead pointed out, Jesus Christ holds the loyalty of people with vastly different ideas about him, all of which contain truth, but none the complete truth, and, though Church creeds have to be voiced communally, their interpretation varies from individual to individual. Yet Jesus never demanded acceptance of a theological proposition as a condition of discipleship. Rather, he gave what the Quakers would call "guiding precepts"—"Follow me ... Go and sin no more ... Do this in memory of me". Nevertheless, he taught with authority, so that people became increasingly infected with his spirit, convictions being born which later developed into their creeds.

In particular, he was at one with the Almighty, even teaching his disciples to address God as "Abba" or "Daddy". In Christ, as in a mirror, we see God reflected, and we, who are all sons and daughters of God, call him THE Son of God. When indicating himself, admittedly, Jesus favoured the modest expression "son of man", which, among Jews, could mean just a man, especially one who was a member of the covenant community. "Son of God" did not, in more erudite circles, necessarily imply being at one with the single true God, but I have been told that there was a popular phrase used to describe a holy man that surely must have been applied to Jesus, which translates roughly as, "He's a real son of God, that chap!" It is with such kind of thoughts in mind that I penned the enclosed hymn, "God's Special Son".

With warm wishes and congratulations!

Hazel Hudson

Hazel's was one among several articles written by contributors to *Worship Live* for the special celebratory fiftieth issue. These offer a lovely warm appreciation of what the community of writers, built up over the years, meant to those who became involved. Her hymn, to which the article refers, appears alongside it.

5. Away in a manger we choose to find Christ

Away in a Manger (revisited)

11.11.11.11 (Anapaestic)	Suggested tune: CRADLE SONG

1. Away in a manger we choose to find Christ,
away from the stresses to keep Christmas "nice";
wrapped up in his stable our Jesus shall stay
so safe and unreal, asleep on the hay.

2. The world bears its suffering—the baby awakes!
So dare we, then, follow? Dare we—as life breaks
and calls us, this Christmas, to seek out God's life
amidst all the tension, the struggles and strife.

3. For God, who is with us, invites us to find
nativity stories re-born in our kind:
revealed at the margins, in tears, God is here—
if only we dare break through faith's binding fear.

Graham Adams

Worship Live has encouraged revisiting traditional texts, to engage the singer in a conversation between what may be much-loved hymns and more recent theologies and world situations. Graham Adams has done this brilliantly here, and in other texts published in *Worship Live* and elsewhere. Gillian Warson looks at another reinterpretation of "Away in a Manger", by Sue Gilmurray, in her *Enjoying Vintage Hymns in Worship: Hidden treasures rediscovered for today's church* (2021, p. 74), and discusses the value of revisiting traditional hymns from a different perspective. Another example by Raymond Vincent is at no. 17 in the current book.

6. Bless the Lord all created things

Bless the Lord all created things
Sing his praise **and exalt him for ever.**

Bless the Lord you sun and moon
Sing his praise **and exalt him for ever.**

Bless the Lord you towering mountains
Sing his praise **and exalt him for ever.**

Bless the Lord you mighty rivers
bless the Lord you raging waterfalls
Sing his praise **and exalt him for ever.**

Bless the Lord you rain and snow
bless the Lord as you water the earth
Sing his praise **and exalt him for ever.**

Bless the Lord you trees and flowers
bless the Lord with your colour and beauty
Sing his praise **and exalt him for ever.**

Bless the Lord you dogs and cats
Sing his praise **and exalt him for ever.**

Bless the Lord you ducks that swim
Sing his praise **and exalt him for ever.**

Bless the Father, the Son and the Holy Spirit:
Sing his praise **and exalt him for ever.**

Jenny Spouge

The author writes:

> I had been going to use a "Song of Creation", e.g. *Hymns & Psalms* (1983, no. 824), [more recently at *Singing the Faith* (2011, no. 791)] or *A New Zealand Prayer Book | He Karakia Mihinare o Aotearoa*, which includes local plants and animals, in an act of worship and then decided it might be better (as it was All Age Worship) to ask those present to make suggestions of their favourite bits of the created world. This was actually in the context of a Christingle Service in which we made the Christingles in stages during the service, so this was in the section on the orange representing the earth and creation. However, it could be used as an act of praise in any service.
>
> So, people (of all ages!) suggested things which were listed on a flipchart:
>
> Flowers, Dogs, Trees, Rivers—big ones, Victoria Falls, Mountains, Cats, Sunshine, Moon, Rain, Snow, Ducks ...
>
> This was then turned into the prayer as we went along, with each phrase ending with "Sing his praise" by the leader, to which the response was "and exalt him for ever".

We were pleased to include several collaborative texts like this. See, for example, no. 76, 83.

7. Bright Sunday's waving palms are fading fast

10.10.10.10　　　　　　　　　　　　　　　Suggested tune: ELLERS

1. Bright Sunday's waving palms are fading fast,
the money-changers' tables are restored,
the faithless crowd's exultant mood has passed,
the Christ-Messiah once again ignored.

2. The Monday morning workplace is prepared.
We turn again to thoughts of everyday
as far away, a crowing bird is heard.
I am not one of his, our actions say.

3. We are the crowd who hail him, scorn him, jeer,
and find his words too full of truth to bear.
We are his friends who in the garden fear
to watch with him, to join with him in prayer.

4. On Friday comes the darkness, comes the end,
his broken body, hanging high above,
compelling us at last to comprehend;
in him we see the true face of God's love.

Carolyn Sanderson

Mike and Carolyn Sanderson were regular contributors to *Worship Live*, mostly writing in their own distinctive voices, but sometimes working together. They were instrumental in developing the writing weekends, which became a feature of the *Worship Live* community, and, in fact, outlasted the publication itself by some time. Mike and Carolyn organized the weekends for many years, in Pershore, and, later, Milton Keynes.

This text attracted a tune, HOLY WEEK, by Basil Bridge, which was published in *Worship Live* issue 46.

8. By a monument of marble

8.7.8.7.D									Suggested tune: LUX EOI

1. By a monument of marble,
or a simple wooden cross,
here we gather to remember
sacrifice and tragic loss.
Blood-red poppy petals flutter,
each a symbol for a life,
drifting in a crimson curtain,
shadow of our constant strife.

2. Solemn silence now surrounds us
as we stand in memory.
Why must factions stir up conflict?
This eternal mystery
troubles hearts and stirs the conscience,
urges us to think again;
face the curse of confrontation,
yet reduce this searing pain.

3. For the sound of war still thunders
through our planet, on this day.
Every hour new victims suffer,
even as we meet to pray.
God, we need your help and guidance
in our constant search for peace.
Move us on to new solutions
as we pray that wars may cease.

Marjorie Dobson

Words © Copyright 2006 Stainer & Bell Ltd. Reprinted by permission.

Marjorie Dobson was a member of the *Worship Live* editorial committee almost from the start, and throughout its life. She was a regular speaker and contributor at our writing weekends. She writes of her own experience in an article in the celebratory fiftieth issue.

This text was part of the response to the sixtieth anniversary of the end of the Second World War. It appeared in Andrew Pratt and Marjorie Dobson, *Poppies and Snowdrops* (2006), in the same year as its publication in *Worship Live*. Since then, it has been included in a number of collections, including the Methodist Church's, *Singing the Faith* (2011), where the present, altered, version is printed. This appears with a new tune, PAPAVER, by Sarah Rodgers, in Dobson's *Unravelling the Mysteries* (2019).

We wrote at the time:

> The sixtieth anniversary of the end of World War II was marked with ceremonies that had an air of finality about them. The generation that lived through the war is now entering the twilight, and there are only ones and twos left of the generation who experienced the Great War . . . Is this an outdated, outworn commemoration or, worse, a reminder of glory days and a glorification of war? Why are the British obsessed with the two World Wars—why are there constant documentaries and books about World War II, in particular?

But the collective memory is still vivid, and the images continue to shock.

9. By grace bestowed, so undeserved

OWLACOMBE (C.M.) Jack Dobbs

The Cup

CM

1. By grace bestowed, so undeserved
by any work of mine,
before my hand is placed a cup
well filled with potent wine.

2. And, though it is my only hope
to drink and understand,
yet fear of leaving self behind
has paralysed my hand.

3. And, though my very heart's desire
is measured in this cup,
yet even so, I lack the strength
to reach and raise it up.

4. O let the spirit now descend
and deep within me flow,
and guide my hand toward the cup
that I may taste and know.

Oliver Leech

Words © Copyright 2000 Stainer & Bell Ltd. Reprinted by permission.

Oliver Leech's disciplined and beautiful text attracted three tunes, which were published together in Issue 20, with comments by Marlene Phillips. Marlene was a member of the editorial committee from the beginning. She brought her musical knowledge to the work, writing tunes to several texts, helping with the selection of music, and as a regular contributor to writing weekends. She wrote short notes or articles on the tunes that we published.

Here, she writes:

> These settings of Oliver Leech's text show how varied the musician's response can be, and yet there are points of similarity. How interesting that each was written in the key of F major, which feels so right. Each composer felt the on-going, unfinished nature of the earlier verses, Jack Dobbs (OWLACOMBE) and Colin Nicholson (THE CUP) finishing each verse with the third of the chord in the melody and Raymond Parfrey writing a broad tune (BY GRACE) which encompasses two verses. In the setting by Jack Dobbs we have a gift for that precious commodity: the four-part choir. Its classic lines and restrained melody, taken at a moderate pace, offer a piece of real beauty.

Jack Dobbs spans the generations with his hymn tunes, including *Congregational Praise* (1951) and *Rejoice and Sing* (1991). We were honoured to include several of his tunes in *Worship Live*.

10. By the light of a flickering lantern

There were three issues of *Worship Live* per year, each of which included a focus on a season of the Christian year. Over the years, we built up an impressive amount of material exploring Advent and Christmas themes from a range of perspectives. This atmospheric text and tune depict the Christmas story like a series of paintings, which draw the eye to the light. The last verse brings the singer into the painting, and into the story.

Christmas Lights

9.10.9.10.5

One or two voices only
1. By the light of a flickering lantern
I can see the babe lying in the straw.
It is cramped and they're cold and weary
but his mother Mary looks down on him
with her face aglow.

Women only
2. By the light of a thousand angels
I see shepherds high in the fields above.
When they hear what the herald's saying
they run down the hill into Bethlehem
with their hearts on fire.

Men only
3. Men are travelling through the country
with their gazes fixed on a shining star.
When they reach where the child is living
they bow down and offer him gifts of gold,
frankincense and myrrh.

4. *Instruments only*

All
5. By the lights of so many churches
we see people praising the living Lord,
for they know it's not just a story
and the Christmas child is the Son of God
and his name is love.
Repeat last line, men only, then women only.

Janet Lancefield

11. Caedmon

The gift of Caedmon
Caedmon
the silent one
on the edge of the group—
contributing nothing.
Doing his job
caring for the animals,
close to creation maybe
but in human company
nothing—
putting himself down.

Hilda
holding together
a whole community—
amid all that activity
all those words
how can she be expected
to hear the silences
of men, women
who feel alone, unused, disabled—
the gaps through which God is falling?

But God comes to earth here:

in Caedmon inspired
to tell the story of Salvation
to sing of Creation
from where he stands with his feet on the ground . . .

and in Hilda's gift of hearing
the song in his silence,
seeing the possibility
of his becoming fully
the person God made him to be.

Giving God, may all our communities
be gifted like this:
with his creativity
and her encouragement.

Jan Sutch Pickard

This text was written at the Conference, "Towards the Promised Community", held in 1998 at Ushaw, near Durham, to mark the end of the WCC Decade for the Churches in Solidarity with Women. Hearing people into speech and song has been one of the great gifts of women's empowerment in recent years.

Hilda (Abbess Hild) and Caedmon's story appears in a panel on a new icon commissioned by The Council of Churches for Britain and Ireland (now CTBI), painted by Edith Reyntiens, and dedicated at the Conference. Reyntiens wrote about the spiritual and artistic discipline of icon painting, and the complex relationship between her subject matter and the tradition of iconography in an ecumenical setting, in an article in the same issue of the journal (Issue 18). The icon was installed in the chapel of the nine altars in Durham Cathedral, where it can still be seen.

12. Can you trace the pattern of the rays of the sun?

STAFFA (12.11.12.13)
Christopher Humphries

Unusually, we gave a whole year's issues to the theme of the Trinity, one issue to each aspect. This gave the opportunity to explore the nature of God in great depth, and we found that at the end of the year we needed a fourth issue to consider the delights of a trinitarian God. This text demonstrates the creativity that developed through this long period of exploration, uncovering encounter with God through human senses and experience.

The Rays of the Sun
12.11.12.13

1. Can you trace the pattern of the rays of the sun,
scattering the shadows now the day's begun?
Can you hear the song of life below and above,
as it tunes us to the praises of the God of love?

2. Do you feel the breaking of the bread in our hands,
nourishing, sustaining us for life's demands?
Do you sense the sharing with the Saviour of all,
as he gathers those together who will hear his call?

3. Will you breathe the Spirit, blowing wild, blowing free,
showing us the people we were meant to be?
Will you face the changes that disturb and renew,
always trusting that his faithfulness will see you through?

4. Melody and harmony that sing to the soul,
sounding notes of joy to touch and make us whole.
Glory to the Trinity, the three that are one,
ever hold us in your unity, 'til time is done.

Christopher Humphries

13. Choosing to return home

The Prodigal Returns
Choosing to return home,
the prodigal fears the encounter,
it's the father he dreads,
not the elder brother.

Choosing to return home,
the prodigal fears the meeting,
it's the father's response he dreads,
not that of the elder brother.

Choosing to return home,
the prodigal fears the reunion,
it's the father's interrogation he dreads,
not the elder brother's verbal outburst.

Choosing to return home,
the prodigal fears the arrival,
it's the father's touch he dreads,
not the elder brother's avoidance.

Choosing to return home,
the prodigal fears the loss of intimacy—
it's "Abba, Father" which is painful bliss
not the elder brother's religious patriarchy.

Frances Ballantyne

Frances Ballantyne was a contributor to *Worship Live* for many years. Several of her texts were later published in anthologies, for example, by Geoffrey Duncan. Many of her prayer poems draw on her own experience in life and church.

She writes:

> I'm a survivor of child-sexual abuse from an elder of the Open Brethren tradition. Many years beyond initial disclosure, working through the process of forgiveness and justice, I had the bitter sweet experience of being in Crown Court when he was convicted and imprisoned. There is a future from that past, God opened up the ordained ministry for me (email, 27 January 2023)

The theme of Issue 38, in which this appeared, was Choices and Turning Points and it featured two poems focusing on the Prodigal Son from different standpoints. The other, by Alan Horner, can be found at no. 3.

14. Clap your hands all you trees!

Albert Jewell and Sylvia Crowther were contributors to *Big Blue Planet* (1995), a collection of songs "for young children to share with each other and with people of all ages". The lively style of this hymn conceals a theological punch, as it links the glorious eschatological promise of Isaiah with the prophetic words of Jesus when they tried to silence the crowds crying out their Hosannas: "I tell you that if these were silent, the stones would shout out."

Hosanna

Irreg. *Based on Isaiah 55:12; Luke 19:38–40*

1. Clap your hands all you trees!
Clap your hands all you trees!
Clap your hands all you trees!
Clap and wave your hands to the Lord!
Hosanna, Hosanna, Hosanna! Praise!
(piano answers)
Hosanna, Hosanna, Hosanna! Praise!

2. Shout out for joy all you hills!
Shout out for joy all you hills!
Shout out for joy all you hills!
Shout out for joy to the Lord!
Hosanna, Hosanna, Hosanna! Praise!
(piano answers)
Hosanna, Hosanna, Hosanna! Praise!

3. Clap your hands all you people!
Clap your hands all you people!
Clap your hands all you people!
Peace on earth and glory to the Lord!
Hosanna, Hosanna, Hosanna! Praise!
(piano answers)
Hosanna, Hosanna, Hosanna! Praise!

4. Shout out in praise all you stones!
Shout out in praise all you stones!
Shout out in praise all you stones!
Shout out in praise to the Lord!
Hosanna, Hosanna, Hosanna! Praise!
(piano answers)
Hosanna, Hosanna, Hosanna! Praise!

Albert Jewell

15. Colliding with God

Accident
Colliding with God,
and wearing no seat-belt,
he suffered extensive injuries
to his life.
They say he is not the same man
since the accident.

God, too, did not escape unscathed,
but received nasty wounds
to his hands and feet,
and a deep laceration in his side.
His condition is said to be critical
and a full recovery
is unlikely.

Neither party
is covered by insurance.

Richard Skinner

This text offers a stark reflection on the encounter between Christ and the Christian, both of whom bear scars. It appears in the issue with two others by Richard Skinner, in which he offers alternative ways of viewing the passion and crucifixion in the light of some of the atrocities and disasters of more recent times. The poem was written in 1983 and appeared in his first collection, *Leaping and Staggering* (1988). More recently it has been included in *Colliding With God* (2017).

16. Come dare to live in the world today

9.9.9.7　　　　　　　　　　　Suggested tune: LONDON (see notes, below)

1. Come dare to live in the world today,
come dare to look at ourselves and say:
"We wonder what is the part we play
to be our neighbour's keeper?"

2. We'll look again at the words we use,
we'll think again of the ways we choose,
to live and heal and not abuse,
and be our neighbour's keeper.

3. We'll think again of all we've been taught,
the way we've spent and the way we've thought,
for some of this is reduced to naught,
when we're our neighbour's keeper.

4. Come dare to love in our world today,
come, for our Maker will firmly say
that each of us has a part to play,
to be our neighbour's keeper.

Anne J. Sardeson

Because it was published three times a year, *Worship Live* could respond reasonably quickly to world events, and often did. This hymn was written in response to the London bombings of 7 July 2005. There was often an unexpected consonance with the issue theme, which would have been set a year or more in advance. As it happened, the issue in which it was published was based on the theme of War and Peace.

A tune, LONDON, is also available; please contact the author via this book's website (see page iii).

17. Come, for everything's ready

Irreg.   Suggested tune: *Sacred Songs and Solos*, no. 405

1. Come, for everything's ready, all the tables are laid.
It's a free invitation, so don't be afraid.
There is food here in plenty and the choicest of wine,
and God's sent out the message, "Come in now and dine."
Come and join the party,
come from near and from far!
God would love you to be there,
whoever you are.

2. We are sometimes too busy with our worries and care,
with jobs and with houses, not a moment to spare.
Life slips by so quickly as year follows year,
and God keeps on calling, but we've no time to hear.
Come and join the party,

3. There are others God calls in their hunger and need,
but we keep them out with our self-serving greed.
We grab the top places and the best of the fare,
but the food will just choke us till we learn how to share.
Come and join the party,

4. So let's go for the real feast for ourselves and for all
and let the world know of God's wide open call.
Go out on the highways and invite them all in,
till the house has been filled and the party can swing.
Come and join the party,

Raymond Vincent

The author writes:

> This is based on an old hymn from *Sankeys* that I used to enjoy singing as a child (Sacred Songs and Solos no. 405). It is based on the Parable of the Feast, but while the original hymn spiritualizes it in terms of personal salvation, I have broadened it out to embrace the idea of sharing in a fuller sense.

Worship Live encouraged new interpretations of old hymns in terms of more recent theologies. Graham Adams revisits another well-loved text at no. 5.

18. Come in to the warmth

10.8.8.8.10   Suggested tune: O JESULEIN SÜSS

1. Come in to the warmth,
come in from the cold,
come, hear the tale of love unfold.
God loved the world with all its pain
and came to earth, its peace to gain.
Come in to the warmth,
come in from the cold.

2. Come in from the wet,
come in to the dry.
New life is in a baby's cry.
This child will grow to set us free
by cruel nails on Calvary's tree.
Come in from the wet,
come in to the dry.

3. Come in to the peace,
come in from the noise.
Restore the Eden that sin destroys.
While God comes gently to the earth,
new hope, new future springs to birth.
Come in to the peace,
come in from the noise.

John Bradley

One way that an author can bring a new context to the singing tradition is to set a hymn to a tune that has a particular resonance. The tune suggested by John Bradley for this text, O JESULEIN SÜSS, is familiar to Percy Dearmer's words, "O little one sweet", based on a German original. Bradley's text brings the singer right in to the biblical context, first the stable, then the cross, and finally Paradise restored. No. 19 demonstrates a similar resonance, but with a very different tune.

19. Come, vast eternal dance of one-in-three

Communion-in-Trinity

10.10.10.10.10.10　　　　　　　　　　　　Suggested tune: SONG 1

1. Come, vast eternal dance of one-in-three,
all-flowing, circling, never standing still,
dynamic web of love exchanged for love,
cascading light that urges on your will:
flow through us here who come to share anew
communion with each other and with you.

2. Earth-making God, you breathe life into dust
to call things into being night and day.
You recreate, repair what we have spoiled,
remake us as a potter shapes the clay.
From all that mars us, heal and set us free:
help us become what you would have us be.

3. Pain-bearing God, you come with wounded hands
to offer lives transfigured and made new,
through body broken, blood and water poured,
and tears that fall for all that's still to do.
Show us that need, the pain that you still bear;
help us respond with action shaped by prayer.

4. Life-giving God, you come through bread and wine,
through Word that's read, proclaimed, enacted, lived;
to fill your people with your various gifts
and send us out to love as Jesus did.
Empower us now, bind us in unity,
in your own image, God-in-Trinity.

Bill Thomas

Words © Copyright 2004 Stainer & Bell Ltd. Reprinted by permission.

Hymn writers often have a traditional tune in mind when creating a text. Sometimes this is simply to keep a metric pattern, or musical cadence to the words. But sometimes the words of the new hymn resonate with older words, familiarly sung to the same tune. Orlando Gibbons' expansive and magnificent SONG 1 has traditionally been sung to John White Chadwick's "Eternal Ruler of the ceaseless round". Bill Thomas uses the stately breadth of the tune, and nods to the earlier text more than once in this hymn to God in Trinity.

No. 18 demonstrates a similar resonance, but with a very different tune.

20. Crying for the world

Words and Music © Copyright 1997 Stainer & Bell Ltd. Reprinted by permission.

The author writes:

> I woke up one cold Christmas morning, heavy in spirit. My husband and son were already excitedly hustling and bustling around the bright lights of the Christmas tree—my son Nathan in particular—eager to begin tearing off the Christmas paper from his small mound of presents. Every now and then they would call to me, "Are you getting up now?"—impatient for the day's festivities to begin. Tears rolled down my face as I gave thought to the warmth I had, the food to eat and the loved ones to care, and then of those who on this Christmas Day were cold, hungry and lonely. It was no longer I, but the very Christ who was crying.

"Crying for the World" was released on a special edition cassette sponsored by MCA records to raise money in aid of UNICEF for its 50th anniversary. The song is also the theme music for a video depicting the work of Peter and Ann Pretorius and the "Jesus Alive" ministries which set up orphanages and feeding programmes in Mozambique and elsewhere.

5.6.6.5.5 & optional refrain

1. Crying for the world,
for all the boys and girls,
crying for the children,
crying for the world,
crying for the world.

Chorus
Oh! Jesus loves us,
Yes he has loved us
Since the beginning of time.
Children are crying,
Children are dying,
Children of the divine.

2. Crying for the world,
for all the hungry ones,
crying for the children,
crying for the world,
crying for the world.
Chorus

3. Crying for the world,
for all the hurting ones,
crying for the children,
crying for the world,
crying for the world.
Chorus

4. Crying for the world,
for all the homeless ones,
crying for the children,
crying for the world,
crying for the world.
Chorus

5. Crying for the world,
for all the lonely ones,
crying for the children,
crying for the world,
crying for the world.
Chorus

6. Crying for the world,
for all the needy ones,
crying for the children,
crying for the world,
crying for the world.
Chorus

At the end of the song, the author suggests adding lines referring to current conflicts around the world, such as "Crying for the children of Ukraine", "Crying for the children of Syria" etc.. The song can also be sung without the chorus.

Ruthie Thomas

21. Deep in the core of earth

This text appeared in an issue (20), which included themes of creation and wilderness, among hymns setting God's creation in the context of human exploration and science. Two tunes were written in response, appearing in Issue 26: PRIMEVAL SOURCES by Marlene Phillips, and this one, by Tim Barton.

CM   Alternative: CAMBRIDGE

1. Deep in the core of earth,
primeval sources flow,
their cycles ever pressing on
unseen, alive, below.

2. Here on the planet's face
is birth and life and death,
the seasons ever rolling on
with every fleeting breath.

3. Far in the skies beyond
the stars and planets turn,
their every movement set in space,
each with its time to burn.

4. God of the worlds you made,
we offer praise and prayer,
with human need for faith and trust,
and confidence to share,

5. that all the work we do
will harvest in your name—
while life develops, changes, turns,
your love remains the same.

Heather Phillips

22. Deep in the heart of God

HEART OF GOD
Marlene Phillips

Words © Copyright 1993, Music © Copyright 1995
Stainer & Bell Ltd. Reprinted by permission.

CMD

1. Deep in the heart of God there lurks
a mischief-making note,
a gurgle of suppressed delight,
a chuckle in the throat.
Deep in the heart of God there lies
a reservoir of pain,
a cross-marked agony of love
filled and refilled again.

2. God of our laughter and our tears,
transcending human thought,
you share our fun in life, our fears,
by incarnation brought:
Father of Jesus Christ, the clown,
whose Spirit gives us breath,
hear us, who look to you to crown
our merriment, our death.

"In God are Remembrances of the broken hearted clown"

Ian Fraser

Ian Fraser was a hugely influential figure at the start of the "Hymn Explosion" of the 1960s–1970s, a prime mover in the organisation of the Dunblane consultations in the 1960s. We were proud to feature a number of his texts in *Worship Live* over the years, many of which offer a sideways look at familiar biblical concepts. "Deep in the heart of God" appeared first in *Try-It-Out Hymnbook* (1995), set to Donald Rennie's tune BROKEN HEARTED CLOWN, and found its way into the first post-launch issue of *Worship Live* in the summer of that year.

We always hoped that new texts would attract new tunes, and this tune by Marlene Phillips appeared in that autumn's issue. She wrote a short article about setting the text, in which she comments:

> My first reaction was that it needs space and freedom in the setting to accommodate its varied rhythms and moods. The tune therefore hangs between major and minor and aims to follow the rhythm of the words.
>
> Problems spring from the felicities of this poem. "Chuckle" in v. 1 has to be a "scotch snap", but one can hardly use the same rhythm for "incar-nation" in v. 2. So v. 2 needs this section writing out separately. I had to remind myself that this was a hymn and not a through-composed song, and that in most hymns there are huge mood swings and huge variations in the number and stressing of syllables, all accommodated by one tune... However, this was FUN to set.

23. Don't forget your lunch box

Schoolday
13/3/96

"Don't forget your lunch box,
and your kit bag for P.E.,
or to draw a lovely picture
to show to Dad and me—
have a happy day,
I'll be waiting here at three,
and if you're very lucky
we'll have chocolate cake for tea!"

Then in stalked Death,
with storm-brained lunacy
and scythed their sweetness down . . .
In vengeful wrath was mayhem wrought,
and deafening abuse—

Till sudden silence fell upon the space
where in the fearful day's eclipse
lay Hell let loose.

Sorrow and pain remain within the place
as Evil's poisonous legacy . . .

For who could ever dry that blood-wet floor?

Margot Arthurton

We were pleased to include poems by Margot Arthurton in *Worship Live*, almost from the beginning of its life. Many of these were written in response to current events, as this one, which refers to the massacre of children in Dunblane in 1996. It appeared in one of the first issues of *Worship Live*, in Summer 1996, when the tragedy was fresh in our minds. The issue focused on "The Valley of the Shadow", including material on Bosnia and Chernobyl, including a lovely image by Kathy Priddis on the front cover, and another poem by Margot Arthurton, "At the Ceasefire", from "Fragments of War and Peace" (Bosnian Arts Project, 1995).

24. Early Easter morning—all were sunk in fear

Hymn for Eastertide

11.11.10.11   Suggested tune: NOEL NOUVELET

1. Early Easter morning—all were sunk in fear:
three years in his company, now he was not here.
Soon to each person Jesus was revealed—
different questions answered, different sorrows healed.

2. Why was Mary weeping, kneeling by the cave
mourning her dear Master, taken from the grave?
Then, close behind her, Risen Jesus came
and, with real compassion, gently called her name.

3. Why was Peter running? John had raced ahead.
Could they trust a woman? 'Christ's not there', she'd said.
There in the tomb the empty grave clothes lay.
Dazed, yet half-believing, Peter walked away.

4. Why was Thomas missing? He was filled with gloom;
could not face the others in that upper room.
Knowing his turmoil, Jesus sought him out;
showed his scars and nail wounds; left him in no doubt.

5. Why are we rejoicing at this Eastertide?
We can never see his blood-stained hands and side.
Yet we are bidden, 'Do not weep and grieve,
blest are you who see not, yet who still believe.'

6. So we come with gladness, not with gloom or fear.
Jesus Christ is risen; he is with us here.
Still to each person, lovingly revealed—
different questions answered, different sorrows healed.

Margaret Walker

By the time this hymn was written, our writers' weekends had been running for a decade or so, and had settled into a pattern of amazing creativity and output. Margaret used the opportunity to revise a hymn written at one of the earlier weekends, and to pen this new text on the theme of resurrection appearances. She writes: "Looking at the Bible, I was struck by the way in which Jesus dealt with his disciples in differing ways—each according to his or her need. He still does that today. He call us by our name and knows our individual needs."

25. Founder of the laws of motion

Hymn for the New Year

8.7.8.7D Suggested tunes: ABBOTS LEIGH or BLAENWERN

1. Founder of the laws of motion,
Lord, who set our world in space,
gave us sun and moon and ocean,
measures of our lives' brief pace:
may this time the year is turning
prompt us all, in you to find
fresh perspectives, in our learning
of your gifts to humankind.

2. For the zeal of exploration,
for our science and our art,
all that sets, within creation,
work of human mind apart,—
thanks we give in celebration
of our forebears' deeds and fame.
Make us, in our generation,
worthy of our human name.

3. So we beg to be forgiven
all that puts our race to shame:
torture; souls from homelands driven;
acts of war that kill and maim;
squand'ring of the earth's resources;
wealth maintained at cost to poor;
blind abuse of nature's forces—
conscience ever more unsure.

4. Lord, our count of years we reckon
from the sending of your Son.
Make the coming years which beckon
richer still than those now done:
rich in wisdom, rich in caring,
rich in harmony and peace;
in the love of Jesus sharing
hope and joy which shall not cease!

Roger Tabor

St Paul's Cathedral ran a competition to find a new hymn to celebrate the Millennium. Hymns were to be trinitarian in structure, and in the metre 8.7.8.7D. The winner was chosen and celebrated, and plans were made for a collection of the best submissions to be published as a book. Unfortunately, this did not prove possible, but there are a number of wonderful hymns in this rousing metre now in use as a result. Roger Tabor's was selected for the publication, and his exciting and challenging text needed only a few alterations to bring it into use as a hymn for all times.

26. Gentle to understand

Gentle to understand, gentle to take my hand,
caring for folk who live in fear.
Gentle to choose a word, gentle until it's heard,
patience will speak out-loud of love.

Louise Counsell

The issue editor writes:

Louise's contribution to the writing weekend at Rydall Hall in 2014 was invaluable. It was lovely to have her advising on tune writing and also accompanying our singing on her violin. She composed this short, simple song at the weekend and added the harmony at a later stage.

All the hymns written at the weekend were sung at our Communion service at the end. Louise's song featured as a sung response to prayers that can be found later in this issue of *Worship Live*.

27. Go canny Brother Aidan! Iona's rocks are sharp

Landfall with Columba, AD 563
Go canny Brother Aidan! Iona's rocks are sharp
as thorns of Christ! Follow the seals!
See? There! Where foam opens its mouth
like a great fish that gulps for breath!
Steer away! Look to a lapping shore!

Ready with the rope brothers! Steady!
Lord, on this barren isle we will stonebuild
to the mystery of Christ and your glory.
By your will these pagan lands shall know
the true way of the risen Christ.

Under a raintight roof I'll take
first flight feathers from the left hand wing
of my Irish swan for strength and living grace.
I'll sharpen quills and write the rounded script
that best sets down Christ's Gospels.

Day and night by candleglow will I labour
with pen and goldleaf to illuminate
the beauty of half uncials, and joyful capitals.
By my handswork shall Christ's deeds crest
like a tidal wave to carry lost souls
to the haven of your perpetual glory.

My book shall be the humble boat
that bears the word of the living Christ
and my quill a rudder to Heaven.
By your mercy
we mission the mainland.

Brothers! Shout to the Lord! Shout!
Let news of our landing fly up like gulls
that others come after us and we prosper!
O grant us long life to do your work
and bless this white rock we step on.

Lord,
let us find water.

Maggie Norton

Worship Live encouraged interaction with our Christian heritage, and we celebrated a number of historic figures in our pages. Maggie Norton's stirring poem, with its strong sense of place, arises from her interest in the history of North-Western Britain, and particularly the churches of Cumbria. She was appointed Poet Laureate of South Lancashire for 2007, during which time, she writes: "I travelled to read abroad and here in England, was translated into Italian and Romanian, and had a wonderful time." In her notes on the poem, she mentions two local churches dedicated to St Cuthbert, "twelfth century founded, and some even older, and some rumours of saints travelling from Ireland landing on Piel Island and walking through the old drove roads to the northern passes", as well as her own parish church, which is "very old, with connection to Furness Abbey" (emails, 5 and 27 January 2023). Columba's landfall is very much part of this heritage.

28. God became a man in Jesus

God in Jesus

8.7.8.7.D Trochaic   Suggested tune: AUSTRIA

1. God became a man in Jesus;	*John 1:14*
see God's power in him displayed;	*Acts 2:22*
see as well his human weakness—	
one of those whom he had made.	*John 1:10 Hebrews 2:17*
Both his natures fully blended:	*cf. Creed of Chalcedon*
perfect God and perfect man.	
He's unique, there's no-one like him:	*Luke 1:26–37 Acts 4:12*
God confined to human span.	

2. God incarnate showed his power	
in his miracles of love,	*e.g. Mark 1:29–34*
in his teaching and debating	*e.g. Matthew 21,22*
showing wisdom from above.	
God incarnate shared our frailty,	
in the rhythm of his days,	
working hard and sometimes resting;	
humble service marked his ways.	*John 13:2–17*

3. Tyrant of this world we live in,	*John 12:31*
Satan held his kingdom fast;	
sparring with Messiah Jesus	*e.g. Matthew 4:1–11*
till he saw his chance at last:	
Satan entered into Judas,	*Luke 22:3*
moved him to betray his Lord,	*Luke 22:6*
moved the world to kill its Saviour,	*Luke 22:2*
promised each their own reward.	*Luke 22:2,5*

4. Came the battle of the ages　　*John 12:31–33*
God in Christ reached out to save;　*2 Corinthians 5:19*
Satan, using men recruited,　　　*Luke 22:3*
killed and sealed God in the grave.　*Matthew 27:45–50,65,66; Acts 20:29*
Exercising mighty power　　　　*Ephesians 1:19,20*
God in Jesus broke death's cords,
rose, ascended, now in splendour　*Acts 2:32,33*
rules victorious, Lord of lords.　　*Revelation 19:16*

Hugh G. Wetmore

Hugh Wetmore, a hymn writer from South Africa, founder of the Evangelical Fellowship of South Africa, and Evangelical Seminary of South Africa, was a frequent contributor to *Worship Live*. His hymns were always soundly biblically based, and nearly always annotated with specific biblical texts, as here. Over the years, he built a close working relationship with the composer Hazel Hudson, whose article on writing for *Worship Live* appears at no. 4. It was a delight to see collaborations developing across continents through the pages of *Worship Live*.

29. God of love and grace

For a retirement

6.6.6.6.8.8   *Well done, good and faithful servant* (Matthew 25:21)

1. God of love and grace,
whose fearsome powers extend
beyond all time and space,
we dare to call you friend
for each and everyone you call
with 'follow me' to one and all.

2. Your service teaches truth
and makes us free indeed.
Help us, in age or youth,
to meet our neighbour's need:
and may our gentle Saviour still
give strength to know
    and do your will.

3. On this thanksgiving day,
which marks a race well run,
your people meet to say,
"Dear friend(s) in faith, well done! *
Your Master knows the busy years
lived out in joy and toil and tears."

4. We promise here and now
to serve our whole life long.
Accept the solemn vow
we make in prayer and song.
Dear Lord, the past is truly blessed,
let future ventures be the best!

* names may be substituted if they fit the metre: e.g. "Dear June and John, well done!"

John Coutts

John Coutts served on the editorial committee for many years, including some time on the northern committee when we worked geographically for a while (see Preface). A prolific writer, producing down to earth, sometimes humorous, always deeply compassionate texts, including poems and sketches as well as hymns, he appears in many issues of *Worship Live*. This lovely hymn for a retirement attracted a tune by Paul Hughes, which was published a year or so later, in issue 45.

30. God of my faith, I offer you my doubt

Andrew Lane

Colin Ferguson has been a regular contributor to *Worship Live* over the years. He describes his hymns as "more human than holy" because of his experience as a probation officer (interviewed for *WL* issue 59). He attended our writing weekends and, when Covid put an end to face to face gatherings, continued their life through "Words for Worship" online. This hymn appeared in his own collections of hymns, most recently, *Dare to Believe* (2018) and has found a place in *Singing the Faith* (2011), along with others of his hymns.

God of my all
10.10.10.10

1. God of my faith, I offer you my doubt,
for life at times seems far too dark for me
and my belief becomes more insecure
when worldly cares produce uncertainty.

2. God of my hope, I offer you my fear,
when I am scared by my anxiety,
when all I hear is suffering and woe,
in all my shadows you will walk with me.

3. God of my joy, I offer you my grief,
when I sink down in sadness or despair,
when in depression I cannot be touched,
I pray in all my depths to find you there.

4. God of my love, I offer you my pain,
when I'm alone and feel nobody cares,
in aching age or in rejected youth,
you bear my cross and dry my human tears.

5. God of my life, I offer you my dreams,
light in the darkness when I hide from view,
light in my faith, my hope, my joy and love,
light in my life and all my life in you.

Colin Ferguson

31. God of the galaxies spinning in space

© 1992 Hope Publishing Company, www.hopepublishing.com.
All rights reserved. Used by permission.

From the start of *Worship Live,* we featured writers and resources that were influencing worship development. An early example was Shirley Erena Murray, whose hymns were already introducing fresh themes, such as environmental concerns, and spreading the net of inclusivity in the language of hymnody. "God of the galaxies" had appeared in *In Every Corner Sing* (1992) and *Alleluia Aotearoa* (1993), and we were delighted to include it in one of our earliest issues (1:2).

10.10.10 & refrain

God of the galaxies spinning in space,
God of the smallest seed, our living source:
yours is the gift of this beautiful place—

Refrain: Let us care for your garden and honour the earth.

Careless and covetous, gross are our greeds
taking the riches the garden provides,
wasting its goodness, forgetting its needs,

Refrain: Let us care for your garden and honour the earth.

Forests and rivers are ravaged and die,
raped is the land till it bleeds in its clay,
silenced the birdsong and plundered the sea—

Refrain: Let us care for your garden and honour the earth.

Let there be beauty and let there be air
fragrant with peace, never poisoned with fear,
freed from the plagues of pollution and war,

Refrain: Let us care for your garden and honour the earth.

Life is a holy thing, life is a whole,
linking each creature and blessing us all,
making connections of body and soul.

Refrain: Let us care for your garden and honour the earth.

Shirley Erena Murray

32. Great is God's truth, it shall prevail

Amnesty
LM

1. Great is God's truth, it shall prevail
through storm and lightning, wind and hail.
A silent flame within a wire
rebukes the self-promoting liar.

2. A wire imprisons, tortures, chills,
oppresses, terrifies and kills.
Grey, like the dusk of evil's hour,
and twisted, like distorted power.

3. A flame, truth's messengers have lit;
no human hand can darken it.
Its light shines on around the earth
asserting every human's worth.

4. A flame to frighten, yet inspire,
this silent flame within a wire.
Great is God's truth, it shall prevail
and tyrant and dictator fail.

David Mowbray

© David Mowbray/Jubilate Hymns. Administered by The Jubilate Group, Kitley House, St Katherines Road, Torquay TQ1 4DE, copyrightmanager@jubilate.co.uk.

A well-established hymn writer, David Mowbray often sent his texts to *Worship Live*, and we were pleased to include them. This hymn is based on the Amnesty International Logo, depicting a lit candle in a coil of barbed wire (see also Sheila Baldock's hymn at no. 55). The hymn, like the logo, is stark. The language is terse and contained, and the hymn returns to its trust in truth over tyranny, ending where it began.

33. Held captive by the king of love

CMD   Suggested tune: LADYWELL

1. Held captive by the king of love,
my life shall then be free
and I shall roam my prison cell
of vast eternity.
My feet held fast, I'll run your race
across eternal years;
my hands held captive by your grace
shall wipe away all tears.

2. The seal of love upon my mouth
shall make it burst in song,
so shall I sing your glory, Lord,
your mark upon my tongue
and blinded by your glory, Lord,
I'll see you on your throne
and though my heart is chained by you
your blessed self I'll own.

3. Held captive by your grace and love,
true freedom I shall know,
held fast by you I shall go forth
your hidden self to show,
to show your grace, to show your love
that my glad heart has bound,
thus free from self yet held by you
is all my freedom found.

Ambrose D. Wright

Words © Copyright 1997 Stainer & Bell Ltd. Reprinted by permission.

There is a wonderful paradox at the heart of Christian discipleship, aptly encapsulated in Cranmer's phrase: "whose service is perfect freedom" (in the collect for peace, for example). Ambrose Wright's carefully constructed text explores the experience contained in these words in a series of vivid images. It appeared in an issue (2.3) on travelling worship, where it provided a still centre, before sending the singer out to show God's grace, that both binds and frees.

34. Holy Spirit hovering, brooding

8.7.8.5D

1. Holy Spirit hovering, brooding
over ancient waters deep,
as the word of God creating,
called our souls from sleep.
Holy Spirit, re-creating,
fills us with eternal life.
Power transforming,
   love reshaping
darkness into light.

2. Holy Spirit, testifying,
whispers we are born of God;
children of a heavenly Father,
circled by his love.
Holy Spirit, searching, knowing
all God's mind, his
   deepest thought,
guides us into truth, revealing
wisdom, Spirit taught.

3. Holy Counsellor, advisor,
making known the Saviour's life;
clarifying all his sayings,
glorifying Christ.
Holy Advocate, defender,
with God interceding still,
forms our praying, moulds
   our longing,
blends it to God's will.

4. Holy Spirit, liberating,
frees our souls from sin and death;
joy and peace and hope releasing,
deepening our faith.
Holy Spirit, generous, giving
power to witness, gifts to serve,
works inspiring, love igniting,
strengthening the Church.

Ruth Buckley

Words and music work together in this hymn to the Holy Spirit. The running quavers of the melody carry the singer from verse to verse. It is good to see a text exploring the Spirit as creator, witness and counsellor. The tune doesn't pause, but moves on from verse to verse, until the final lines of the fourth verse lead the singer through a lively celebration of the fruits and gifts of the Spirit to burst upwards to reach the top of the scale in "strengthening the Church".

35. Hopkins, your bright kestrel

Great Orme, Advent Sunday
(*After Gerard Manley Hopkins' poem* The Windhover)

Hopkins, your bright
kestrel horseman rode the air,
challenged the wind.

Mine held above my head,
hunched, head down,
fierce hunter, watching
the tangled turf and gorse,
shrugging wings' shoulders,
impatient of the wind—
then, with a swerve and slip
deep into the blue sky and
down again to another sharp watch.

Which is the hunter? Am I
still hunting the hidden God in the tussocks,
blown away by the wind?

Or is God
watching me, head bent,
beak and claws ready to rend,
waiting for me to break cover,
but sliding away when I think I've spotted him?

Patient to pounce only when I say yes?

John Lansley

Through the years, *Worship Live* published a number of hymns by John Lansley. This powerful poem appeared in the anniversary issue (Issue 50). It is written for Advent Sunday and engages the author's personal experience of faith with a poem by Gerard Manley Hopkins.

36. How are we to sing our songs to you?

David Lee

9.9.9.9D

1. How are we to sing our songs to you
when around us lies a world in pain,
when the threat of terror looms so near
and the pace of life brings endless strain?
Men How are we to sing our songs to you?
Women How are we to sing our songs to you?
All How are we to sing our songs to you?
Is this all that we can hope to do?

2. We will sing our songs, the songs that cry
of a world that aches to understand:
of the strife-torn home, the lonely child,
the untimely death, the ravaged land;
Men we will sing our songs, and so express
Women we will sing our songs, and so express
All we will sing our songs, and so express
a lament for this world's brokenness.

3. We will sing our songs, for in those songs
we can feel the echoes of your care,
for the words tell how you walked this earth
and your death reached deeper than despair:
Men at the crux of history, you stepped in
Women at the crux of history, you stepped in
All at the crux of history, you stepped in
to destroy in full the scourge of sin.

4. How can we not sing our songs to you?
When disaster strikes, you keep control;
and you bind the searing wounds of grief
with the hope of worlds new-made and whole:

Men	we will trust you, praise you, come what may;
Women	we will trust you, praise you, come what may;
All	we will trust you, praise you, come what may;
	we will sing our songs to you today.

Martin E. Leckebusch

Words © 2010 Kevin Mayhew Ltd, Buxhall, Stowmarket,
Suffolk, IP14 3BW. Used by permission.

July 2005 saw the announcement of the London Olympics, followed a day later by a devastating series of bombs on the London Underground and Bus services. Martin Leckebusch's hymn appeared in the autumn issue of *Worship Live* (Issue 33), a few months after the events, having already proved useful as a response to tragic events, set to the tune, SING OUR SONGS, written for the hymn by David Lee. Both Martin and David are established writers, whose work is published widely. We have been pleased to include David Lee's tunes in a number of issues of *Worship Live* over the years.

Commenting recently on the tune, David notes that, "Writers sometimes revisit and revise their texts and tunes. In the chorus-like section here, in the line marked for '*All*' at the words 'we to sing', I would now revise the rhythm, simplifying it to match their earlier instances in '*Men*' and '*Women*' lines (three notes: Eb, Eb, Eb-octave), with this '*All*' occurrence becoming simply: Eb, Eb, C."

37. How did it come to this?

Judas
How did it come to this?
One thing's certain: no-one will ever name their son for me.
Who would want to give their child the name of a traitor?
The thing is, I was so angry with him, so frustrated!
For three years I'd followed him,
listened to all his talk about the kingdom,
the establishment of a new world order,
and last Sunday, well, it seemed as if it were about to happen.
You should have seen and heard them!
Lining the streets, cheering him on,
shouting for the Messiah, the Son of David.
And then you should have seen and heard *him* in the temple,
driving out the traders,
not caring about the reaction of the Sadducees
or their Roman masters.
"At last!" I thought, "This is it!"
But then things seemed to change;
he even seemed to support the Roman tax,
"Give to Caesar what's due to Caesar."
Nothing! That's what's due to Caesar.
I see that now, of course,
but at the time, I couldn't believe my ears!
I was furious, couldn't bear to think
I might have wasted three years
following a false Messiah.
But it wasn't revenge that made me go to the Sanhedrin,
though I daresay some will think so.
It wasn't greed either, after all,
thirty pieces of silver is hardly a fortune,
just the going price for a slave killed by accident—
although there was nothing accidental about *his* death—
the Sanhedrin had it all planned.

No, I thought I could force his hand,
thought when he was finally up against it
he'd take decisive action.
Now I've had time to reflect, I know I misread the signals.
Yes, Zechariah had prophesied
about the king riding on a donkey,
but a king coming in peace, not war.
I knew I'd got it wrong in the garden.
When I greeted him he looked at me
with such sorrow and compassion in his eyes.
I'd seen him look like that at others, so many times before,
a look that said, "You're forgiven."
But after what I'd done, how could he forgive me?
If only I could turn back time!
If only I could have my time over again!

Janet Pybon

Storytelling lies at the heart of worship, as we respond to the wealth of sacred story in scripture, and the diversity of human life. From time to time, we received material looking at these stories in new ways, from new perspectives. In Issue 45, whose theme was Storytelling, we published two poems by Janet Pybon: one a meditation on the experience of the tenth bridesmaid, excluded from the wedding feast; the other, this one, the betrayal of Jesus from the standpoint of Judas, the betrayer. Both are stories of regret, by outcasts from the great story of salvation.

38. I believe in God, Creator, Image maker

Creed of a Speech and Language Therapist
I believe in God, Creator, Image maker;
by whom the gift to communicate is given.
From the world's first day to endless eternity,
as the world spins round,
so God continually communicates with us.

I believe in Jesus Christ, Mary's child;
in whom the struggle to communicate is affirmed.
Crucified and Risen, as the Disabled One,
his body, the Church, is a disabled body,
for whom the struggle to communicate is a daily reality.

I believe in the Holy Spirit, Sophia, Wisdom,
by whom all our communication is enlivened.
She calls from street corners—
as loudly outside the church as from within
making every day a feast of Pentecost.

I believe in us all,
called to communicate
faith, hope and love
by breath and body,
word and wisdom,
sign and symbol,
message and machine.
In the embrace of the Holy One
I seek the fullness of life for all.

Janet Lees

In the early years of *Worship Live,* we published or reprinted a number of creeds and mission statements. These emerged not from high level Christian councils, aiming to define the faith for their constituencies, but from the living discipleship of Christians or communities. What is it like to be a Christian living *this* life, or in *these* circumstances? Janet Lees, an ordained minister and speech therapist (also a lecturer in speech and language therapy), wrote about her life and experience in introducing this creed. She said that she was "challenged to integrate all these aspects of [her] life . . . on a daily basis". Her creed is a tour de force of integration, and, in achieving this, speaks into all human life.

39. I wish that my eyes were fountains of tears

Many Tears: One Sorrow

I wish that my eyes were fountains of tears,
then I would weep for my people who were slain.

From Jeremiah 9:1

This intercessory response was written for a "Window on the World" Council for World Mission Conference at the Hayes Conference Centre in Swanwick in 1996. Janet Wootton and Carole Ellefsen-Jones were leading conference worship. They decided to use Jeremiah 9:1 as a prayer response at a worship session focusing on lament. Carole undertook to write a tune, and did so overnight, ready for prayers the next day. Jeremiah's powerful text arises from his identity with those who are suffering, "my people". It can be sung unaccompanied, though the changing chords at the end are then, of course, lost.

40. I wonder, might Joseph

Peter Sharrocks

Worship Live published a number of hymns by Lilian Butler over the years. This text imagines the anticipation of the birth of Mary's child within the family, in all the little practical preparations that mean so much. All this potential exists in every new birth, and feeds into our expectation of the Christ child. Peter Sharrocks has a long career of writing often challenging words and tunes in the folk idiom. He has written tunes to words by Andrew Pratt and Fred Kaan, and, as here, Lilian Butler. Peter was a frequent and valued contributor to our writing weekends.

Wondering

6.6.11.6.6.11

Alternative tune: ASHGROVE

1. I wonder, might Joseph
have fashioned a cradle
employing his skill in the carpenter's trade:
like any new parent,
awaiting the advent,
creating a welcome with something home-made.

2. I wonder did Mary
prepare little garments
while fear and excitement disturbed her in turn.
And did she imagine
her own little stranger
with one of those garments, the day he was born?

3. Elizabeth maybe
allowed cousin Mary
to hold John, her baby, soon after his birth:
and did they both realize
how wonderfully precious
a God-given child is, a joy of our earth?

4. A new life expected
can hold such potential,
the hopes and the visions of things to attain.
We pray that each Advent
provokes us to wonder,
to live for the coming of Love once again.

Lilian Butler

41. I wouldn't touch him with a bargepole

I wouldn't touch him with a bargepole,
this man who broke my family.
How happy we were, safe and calm by the lake.
Each day the boats went out,
a close band of brothers and friends,
fishing for what would feed
and put bread on the table.
The biggest danger was the storms.
Boats tossed before the wind.
But skilful sailors knew
how to ride the waves
and come safe home.

But now the harbour's gone.
A day like any other saw
Jesus walk beside the lake,
call the fishermen to follow him.
And they did! Why?
They weren't foolhardy youngsters.
Simon never gave his family
a second thought. Off he goes.
Wondering, learning—a disciple
he says. Not a husband, that's for sure.
Nor a fisherman any longer.
How will we live, my daughter and I?
I rue the day that man passed our way.
My stomach churns, my heart beats fast.
All is worry and uncertainty.
My fretting has made me ill,
a fever grips me and I toss.
Simon comes; he will bring the Master.
My head shakes, I will not welcome him.

But too weak to move, I lie and wait.
Jesus comes, a calm and strength
fills the room, peace fills me.
I look into his eyes and see no threat.
Only love and concern.
My brow is touched, coolness comes.
All is calm; I feel no fear.
I look to the future and know
for certain that Simon Peter must go
where the Lord leads; we left at home
will also trust his love and care.

Hilary Jackson

The Gospels provide a gripping narrative of ordinary lives overturned by the presence of Jesus as he journeyed among them. He had huge impact on the disciples he called to journey with him, but also on those he healed, and sent back to, or left with their families, to pursue their journeys of discipleship where they lived. We often don't know the names of the "bit part" players, many of them women. This poem, with its arresting first few lines, describes the encounter between Jesus and the mother-in-law of impetuous Peter, who was healed as Peter was called.

42. Imagine a world where our leaders aren't liars

Imagine a World

12.11.12.11　　　　　　　　　Suggested tune: THE BARD OF ARMAGH

1. Imagine a world where our leaders aren't liars,
distorting, reporting and spinning the news;
where all whistle-blowers and brave Jeremiahs
are lauded, applauded and never abused.

2. Imagine a world where believers aren't fighting
and shedding our blood in the name of their gods;
where faith is delightful, enlightening, inviting,
and never deployed for crusades or jihads.

3. Imagine a world where the markets aren't idols,
bowed down to and worshipped in envy and greed;
where wealth is released and the bankers are bridled,
the poor have a plot and the famished a feed.

4. Imagine a world where there is no pollution,
the air is so clear and the oceans are clean;
where humans don't threaten the earth's evolution,
the animals flourish and forests are green.

5. Imagine a world as the Lord has intended,
where goodness and justice and beauty preside;
a world we have broken that might yet be mended:
the future is now, it is ours to decide.

Kim Fabricius

The first line of this hymn calls forth an instant response, even more so, as the twenty-first century moves inexorably onwards, than in the summer of 2005 when it was published in *Worship Live*. The Summer issue often looked to Harvest, One World Week and Remembrance, rather than to the major Christian festivals, and the theme of this issue, When Communities Collapse, provided an additional focus on the world as it is today. Kim Fabricius, whose challenging hymns we often included in our pages, calls us to contrast a world of greed and corruption with the world as God intended. By doing so, he recalls the prophetic vision of justice and righteousness, turning from imagining to deciding and doing.

43. In a land that was parched and baked dry by sun

John Piggins

And I saw Jesus
11.8.10.8.8.9.9.7

1. In a land that was parched and baked dry by sun
in its hard heart nothing would grow—
a dam was built because somebody cared
and the water began to flow.
> A man stood up and tilled his crops
> and his babies soon stopped their weeping.
> I looked again at that new-life man
> and I saw Jesus reaping.
> *In so much as you do it to these, said the Lord,*
> *in so much as you do it to these,*
> *in so much as you do it to these, said the Lord,*
> *you do it to me.*

2. In a land where men go away to work
and the women are left to cope,
a kitchen built because somebody cared
lifted them to new heart and hope.
> A wife stood up and learnt to tend
> and her babies grew better looking.
> I looked again at that new-life wife
> and I saw Jesus cooking.
> *Chorus*

3. In a land where children couldn't read or write—
in today's world they had no part—
a school was built because somebody cared
and the learning for life could start.
> A girl stood up and read her book
> and those children new tales were hearing,
> I looked again at that new-life girl
> and I saw Jesus learning.
> *Chorus*

4. In a land that was torn with the noise of war
and the children had swollen bellies,
the world looked on as if nobody cared
and the hell played out on our tellies.
>A boy too weak to stand just hunched
>and the babies were past their crying.
>I looked again at that old-life boy
>and I saw Jesus dying.
>*Chorus*

Jean Silvan Evans

Jean Silvan Evans' words use the challenge of Jesus in Matthew 25 as a refrain, taking seriously the idea of seeing Jesus in the needs of others. Outreach and development are complex matters and the last verse moves beyond the parable, to end with the death of Jesus echoed in the destruction of human life by war and famine.

The text attracted two tunes: IN SO MUCH by Sue Gilmurray, and the one printed here, REDBANK, by John Piggins. Both Jean and John (and Sue) were frequent contributors to *Worship Live*. John often also worked in partnership with Jean Wiggins. One of the delights of our work was to see authors and composers responding to each other's creativity.

Jean Silvan Evans was also a regular contributor to our writing weekends. She comments: "I loved our hymn writing residential meetings. There was always so much support and practical guidance and I always managed to produce a hymn. I was really proud when they were published in *Worship Live!*" (email, 15 August 2022).

44. In affairs of economics

8.7.8.7D

1. In affairs of economics
Prophet Amos spoke the Word;
those who gained from corrupt commerce
closed their ears to what they heard;
money ceased to be a servant,
means of meeting human need,
killed the heart of God's own People
ruled by power of human greed.

2. In affairs of church attendance
Prophet Amos spoke the Word;
those who offered tainted tribute
closed their ears to what they heard:
worship ceased to be a service
offered gladly from the heart,
lacked the sacrificial living,
its essential other part.

3. In affairs of daily leisure
Prophet Amos spoke the Word;
but the constant background music
closed their ears to what they heard:
leisure ceased to be a tonic
recreating soul and mind,
men and women drunk with pleasure
lost the gift of being kind.

4. To the soul of every nation
Prophet Amos speaks the Word;
in our leisure, commerce, worship,
hear the counsel of the Lord:
fear the wrath of holy judgement
self-inflicted by our ways,
let the will of God Almighty
be the ruler of our days.

Bernard Braley

Words © Copyright 1979 Stainer & Bell Ltd and The Trustees for Methodist Church Purposes (UK). Reprinted by permission.

Worship Live was intended as a creative conversation between writers and readers of the texts, so the author offers these alternatives.

- v 1 l 3—those who worked in shop and office
- v 2 l 3—but both priests and foolish people

Another continuing pattern, started here, was the invitation for new tunes to be submitted. And, indeed, a tune by Marlene Phillips was published in the next issue.

Bernard Braley was very much the instigator of *Worship Live* (see Preface). As managing director of Galliard, he had been one of the first in publishing to recognize and promote the hymn revival of the 1960s and 1970s. Many of us (of a certain age) first encountered the lively, challenging songs of the folk revival in the *Faith, Folk and . . .* series of books (1967–9). His influence on twentieth-century hymnody was incalculable. Appropriately, this hymn was in the launch issue of *Worship Live*, in a section which focused on Amos, the first of many biblical focus points over the years.

45. In the dark before the dawn

Basil E. Bridge

FOURTH WATCH

7.7.7.5

1. In the dark before the dawn—
spirits low and strength outworn—
hopes we harboured seem forlorn,
Come, Lord Jesus, come!

2. When our fears and doubts increase,
when our troubles never cease,
when we long to know your peace,
Come, Lord Jesus, come!

3. When the world is racked with fear,
when the day we dread seems near,
then we cry, "O Saviour! Hear!"
Come, Lord Jesus, come!

4. Help us, Lord, to watch and pray;
darkness must at length give way
to the light of Easter day;
Come, Lord Jesus, come!

Basil E. Bridge

We were privileged to include this hymn text and tune by long-established writer/composer Basil Bridge, whose hymns are widely published. It introduces our issue on prayer, worship and discipleship (no. 43), with a prefatory comment by the editor: "Prayer is by no means easy—no-one ever said it would be . . . Amazingly, we know something about Jesus' own prayer life. We know that he would take time to be alone in the wilderness and pray. We know that, at least at the beginning of his ministry, it was Satan he met there, and wrestled with. And what could be more poignant than his prayer at Gethsemane . . . ?" Bridge's hymn is steeped in that experience, echoed in our own wrestling, and met by the promise of Easter.

46. In the silence of the midnight

The issue of *Worship Live* (22), in which this hymn appeared, was focused on the Word of God in creation, prophecy, storytelling and preaching. We were delighted to welcome Bernard Braley, whose brain-child *Worship Live* was, as guest editor. He writes: "At Christian worship, we meet head-on with the Jesus story. Its telling and retelling down the centuries is an essential part of the weekly liturgy. But it is not just a historical story: it is the ongoing story of the resurrected Jesus, alive and active in every generation." Simon Baynes' hymn makes us witnesses of the mysterious events of the first Easter.

A Resurrection Hymn

8.7.6.8.8.8.6 & refrain

1. In the silence of the midnight,
in the stillness of the tomb,
the power of God is working
to drive away the gloom.
Weeping is past, sorrow is gone,
ended the dark, death is undone.
The winding sheet lies where it fell,
the stone is rolled away.

Sing hosanna to God and rejoice in his name!
He has raised from death his only Son.
He has given us life, we are risen with him,
and the present and the past are one.

2. In the early morning garden,
in the hush before the dawn,
the Son of God in glory
stands risen and reborn.
Hope is alive, ended despair,
gone is our doubt, answered our prayer.
The soldiers lie like senseless men,
the tomb is cold and bare.

Sing hosanna to God and rejoice in his name!
He has raised from death his only Son.
He has given us life, we are risen with him,
and the present and the past are one.

3. In the closely guarded chamber,
on the still Emmaus road,
can it be this lonely stranger
is the risen Son of God?
Hearts are on fire; live from the dead!
Known in the sign—breaking of bread.
Our Jesus back with us again,
our Jesus—can it be?

Sing hosanna to God and rejoice in his name!
We will fall in worship at his feet.
It's the body of Christ, the kingdom of God,
where the present and the future meet.

Simon Baynes

47. In the stillness of this moment

Metaprayer
In the stillness of this moment,
Lord, we come to worship you
with many different ideas
about how and why, where and when;
yet sensing through them all
that it was your voice that called us here.

In the stillness of this moment,
Lord, we come to worship you;
and you, in your infinite love and mercy,
accept each one of us.

Silence
In the rush and noise and madness of life,
Lord, we call on you;
knowing only our need;
all our theology lost
in a sea of anxiety, confusion, hope, pain and loss.

In the rush and noise and madness of life,
Lord, we call on you;
and you, in your infinite love and mercy,
hear each one of us.

Silence
In the communion of this hour,
Lord, we bring you our world;
its sickness, its suffering,
our guilt and our grief,
its joy and its beauty.

In the communion of this hour,
Lord, we bring you our world;
and you, in your infinite love and mercy,
laugh and weep with each one of us.

Silence
Take all our prayers, Lord;
our stutterings, our fine words,
and our unspoken, incoherent thoughts;
and use them,
that we and the world in which we live
may find our wholeness in you.
Amen

Mary Elms

Mary Elms writes: "I still remember the first time that I read C. S. Lewis' poem, 'Footnote to All Prayers'. I have passed on the poem many times to those who are struggling with prayer, and there's an element of the same thoughts here. This prayer was used in a healing service where a prayer about prayer was needed." It was a contribution here to a section on discipleship and service, part of an issue (42) on prayer and worship.

48. Journeying on a day of darkness

8.7.8.7D   Suggested tune: MARCHING

1. Journeying on a day of darkness,
utmost failure in the mind,
two disciples meet a stranger,
speak of what they've left behind.
Journey onward, journey forward,
journey from the past to now,
journey from the now to future,
journey to the promised land.

2. Journeying on a day of darkness,
listening to the prophets' voice,
two disciples meet a stranger,
find a reason to rejoice.
Chorus

3. Journeying on a day of darkness,
in the sharing of their meal,
two disciples meet a stranger,
see his risen life made real.
Chorus

4. Journeying on a day of darkness,
in the breaking of the bread,
we, disciples, meet that stranger,
with whose body we are fed.
Chorus

Mike Sanderson

Mike and Carolyn Sanderson were regular writers for *Worship Live*, mostly writing in their own distinctive voices, but sometimes working together. They were instrumental in developing the writing weekends, which became a feature of the *Worship Live* community, and, in fact, outlasted the publication itself by several years. Mike and Carolyn organized the weekends for many years, in Pershore and, later, Milton Keynes.

49. Knowing us from eternity

All our days
LM   Suggested tune: DANIEL

1. Knowing us from eternity,
guarding us from the day of birth,
your love is constant, never fades,
holding us all our days on earth.

2. Throughout our childhood, you are there.
Motherly tending trips and tears,
fatherly, guarding every step,
you share our joys and soothe our fears.

3. And when we come to fly the nest,
you give us courage for the flight,
watch as we soar, to heaven bound,
freed to discover your truth and light.

4. As years advance, then, still we'll know
your generous care, your warm embrace.
Through sun and shadow, still and storm
we are upheld by endless grace.

5. God, who in Christ became like us,
knowing our life in all its ways,
holding us in your open hand—
strengthen us to our end of days.

Stuart J. Brock

Stuart Brock was a valued member of the editorial team for *Worship Live* for a number of years. At that time, most of the team was resident in the north of England or Scotland, and we used to meet in the lovely setting of the Lake District. His hymn traces the Christian's experience of God through the length of human life, and appears in a section on the love of God. It appears in company with a range of poems and hymns on the same theme, drawn from the lived discipleship of our writers.

50. Lady in the Shadows

Throughout the world her husband's name is a byword for suffering, yet in Job's story she rarely gets a mention. It is his story, and she is shown to be remarkably insensitive to his feelings. Equally he is quite oblivious to hers. We don't know what he says to her or if he is able, out of his depressive state, to offer her any words of comfort. She certainly does not console him. Listen to her: "You are still as faithful as ever, aren't you? Why don't you curse God and die!" No wonder Job tells his friends that "God has made my brothers forsake me", and "My wife can't stand the smell of my breath."

Sometimes tragedy can bring couples closer together, but other times people turn from each other. They look only inwards, tormenting themselves with their feelings of sorrow and pain, their unanswered questions and prayers, so they are unable and unwilling to see that others suffer too.

We are not told how Job's wife felt. But remember her loss. Her seven sons and three daughters were killed. Her husband lost his wealth, his social position, the respect of the community, his health and his self-respect. Everything apart from knowing that God is mighty and holy.

Their surviving relatives abandoned them, children and servants became disrespectful and Job's three friends, once they started to talk, did little more than rub salt into the wound.

How difficult it must have been for Job's wife. Who could she turn to? The only people she saw were the unsatisfactory servants. Her children, and therefore her hopes, were dead.

Job, afflicted as he was, was not in such a deep dark painful place, as he still had hope in God. These dreadful things had been allowed, but . . .

For his wife, however, there were no "buts", no hope. Her depression and bitterness must have been torture to bear.

We are not told how she felt when Job's suffering came to an end and his property was restored and his brothers and sisters and former friends "came to feast with him in his house". Nor are we told how she felt about having another seven sons and three daughters. How can children be replaced? At least the daughters are named—she remains, for all time, Mrs Job.

Judi Marsh

Issue 47 of *Worship Live* was looking to the future. As the first decade of the new millennium passed into history, we wanted to explore new themes. Our guest editor was Andrew Pratt, a prolific and frequently challenging hymn writer, and one of the founder members of our editorial committee, part of the publication throughout its life. He writes: "Somehow the church needs to reclaim that prophetic spirit that can enable new adventures of faith, new discoveries of the unfathomable grace and freedom of God." Judi's reflection sets the scene for one adventure of faith in scripture: listening to the anonymous, shadowy figures who exist on the margins of familiar stories. Often these are women, as here. Job and the "friends" steal the limelight, but Job's wife, often pilloried, a figure of fun, suffers terribly. Judi's perceptive retelling allows the Lady in the Shadows to emerge into the light.

51. Let justice roll like waters

7.6.8.6.7.6.8.6

1. Let justice roll like waters
to heal a broken world,
where homeless, poor and hated hurt,
ignored, despised and scorned.
Servant, touch us with your grace,
that love might be our theme;
infuse our world with righteousness—
an ever-flowing stream.

2. Let justice roll like waters
to save a damaged earth;
restored the balance God spoke forth
before creation's birth.
Wisdom, whisper in our hearts
a way to live your dreams;
redeem our world with righteousness
in ever-flowing streams.

3. Let justice roll like waters
to build a lasting peace,
where each shall have a space to be,
a place in God's great feast.
Spirit, sweep us on beyond
the grip of pride's regime;
transform our world with righteousness—
an ever-flowing stream.

Janet Evans

The writing weekends were amazingly prolific. At this one, held at Holland House, Cropthorne, on bonfire weekend, just before Advent, 35 hymns were written by 17 participants. Five of these were sung at Sunday Eucharist at Pershore Abbey and the others "at Holland House Chapel amidst fireworks on the Saturday evening". The report in *Worship Live* says: "It was clear that *Worship Live* plays an important role in developing hymn writing. Many spoke of their initial contact with the publication, and their own growth as writers through contact with its editors—which they, sometimes ruefully, appreciated." Janet Evans' hymn takes its theme from the mighty prophecy of Amos 5:24.

Words and music © Copyright 1990 Stainer & Bell Ltd. Reprinted by permission.

Cecily Taylor's hymns have appeared in a number of Stainer & Bell publications, including *Partners in Praise* (1979), and *Reflecting Praise* (1993). Several appeared in the predecessor to *Worship Live*, *Hymns and Congregational Songs* including this one in 2.2 (1991), and we have been pleased to include her hymns in several issues of *Worship Live*. Cecily Taylor tells her story in *This is our Song* (Wootton, 2010, pp. 313–9), where she records her debt to Stainer & Bell, and Bernard Braley in particular, and fascinatingly sets her own writing in the context of the hymn explosion and its concerns.

Carry me Shepherd

8.7.10.7.9.7.9.7

Chorus
Lift me up on your shoulder, Shepherd,
carry me back to the fold;
don't let me wander again, Shepherd,
don't let me loosen my hold.

1. There where the grass looks inviting—
whispers a promise of gold,
there when the brambles ensnare me, Shepherd,
carry me back to the fold.
Chorus

2. There where a cave looks exciting—
tempting me in from the cold,
there from the darkness and danger, Shepherd,
carry me back to the fold.
Chorus

3. Then I shall hear, reuniting,
news that a Shepherd foretold—
joy that in heaven is ringing as you
carry me back to the fold.

Cecily Taylor

Words and music © Copyright 1990 Stainer & Bell Ltd. Reprinted by permission.

53. Listen! Mary tells the story

8.7.8.7　　　　　　　　　　　　　　　Suggested tune: ALL FOR JESUS

1. Listen! Mary tells the story,
how she found the empty tomb,
saw the angels, glimpsed the glory,
soon forgot the days of gloom.

2. Smell the spices Mary carried
for a final act of care—
who would move the stone, she worried,
till she saw it was not there.

3. Look! We see discarded linen,
know he is no longer here:
Christ was dead, but now he's living
and will surely soon appear.

4. Feel the mood of jubilation
when they saw that it was true:
feel the sense of celebration
when we add our praises too.

5. Taste the bread as it is broken
once at supper with his friends:
now it's given again in token
of the life that never ends.

Janice Anstey

Janice Anstey calls on the singer to experience the resurrection of Jesus with all our senses, as a physical event, ending with the shared touch and taste of communion. The editor's note says: "This is appropriate to the last issue of *Worship Live* in this form (the following issue was the first to appear online only) ... the editorial committee has been hosted by

Marlene Phillips in her Lake District home. We work very hard, sifting and selecting material. But the highlight of the meeting is always when we break for lunch: always a nutritious and generous meal, with home-made bread, which we break together, in fellowship."

54. Lord God, we thank you

A morning prayer giving thanks for the night

Lord God, we thank you
for the stillness of the night
the opal moon
hanging in the silence,
for the resting of bones
for the easing of muscles and joints.
Lord God we thank you
for the stillness of the night.

Lord Jesus, we thank you
for the peace of the night
the tapestry of stars
weaving through the black calm,
for the release from thought
for the respite from stress.
Lord Jesus, we thank you
for the peace of the night.

Holy Spirit, we thank you
for the ending of the night
the advent of the sun
signalling through the darkness,
for the renewal of our spirits
for the revival of our wills.
Holy Spirit, we thank you
for the ending of the night.
Amen

Heather Johnston

The focus of this issue of *Worship Live* (12) was starting points in worship, from gathering for congregational worship, to the intensity of private devotion. Morning prayers have traditionally imaged the night as a time of peril, ending with the coming of day, appropriate, perhaps, to a pre-scientific age. The rich language of this text celebrates it as a time of rest and renewal, experienced amid the wonder of the cosmic order, prelude to the "advent of the sun".

55. Lord Jesus, help us stand

SM

1. Lord Jesus, help us stand
for what is just and right,
where people hurt and cry in pain
let us be by their side.

2. Give us the courage, Lord,
to make up our own mind
(in spite of what our neighbours think)
about the truth we find.

3. And then let us speak out
as you did years before
against those who use power and might
to victimize the poor.

4. Come let us pray for those
in prisons dark and bare,
because they tried to make a world
where all is just and fair.

5. So may we bring them hope;
a candle in the night,
that glows to show that someone cares;
that somewhere there is light.

6. Thus may our anger be
the energy we use
to climb above our apathy
and fight against abuse.

Sheila Baldock

Sheila Baldock began writing, as many do, because she could not find suitable hymns for worship, particularly, for children. She has several hymns in *Sound Bytes* (1999), as well as in *Worship Live* over the years. This text is published in Issue 21, at the start of the new millennium, with a focus on justice. It is rare for a hymn to honour the energy of anger in combating apathy and abuse. The words point to the work of Amnesty International, with its symbol of a candle, bringing light and hope to prisoners of conscience (see also David Mowbray's hymn at no. 32).

56. Love soars where eagles cease to fly

Jenny Canham

8.8.8.4

1. Love soars where eagles cease to fly,
love sounds the grief beneath a sigh,
love never ponders how or why,
love always lives.

2. Love sings when silence chills the air,
love stills when chaos shatters care,
love understands our calm despair,
love always lives.

3. Love enters into joy and pain,
love fills the dead with life again,
love will endure, will still remain,
love always lives.

4. Love joins our hearts and minds as one,
love shares our grief, our joy, our fun,
love works, love's work is never done,
love always lives.

5. Love offers insight to our care,
love breathes compassion through the air,
love thrives when life is foul or fair,
love always lives.

6. Love values colour, light and shade,
love loves the gifts that love has made,
love brightens life, will never fade,
love always lives.

Andrew Pratt

Words © Copyright 1997 Stainer & Bell Ltd. Reprinted by permission.

Andrew Pratt was with the *Worship Live* editorial committee from its very first meetings at Union Chapel in Islington, and right through its life. He is a widely published hymnwriter, and has been active in supporting hymnody in his teaching, research and writing. "Love soars" was written in 1996 as a wedding hymn for his niece and her fiancé, and was published in *Worship Live* in an issue that focused on life events. Originally written to ALMSGIVING (Dykes), it appears in *Roots and Wings* (2010) with a tune LOVE LIVES by Peter Sharrocks.

For her first submission to *Worship Live*, Jenny Canham offers an alternative tune to ALMSGIVING which she wrote in 2010 for Andrew's text. It was sung, introduced by Andrew himself, on the 75th Anniversary of the founding of the Hymn Society of Great Britain and Ireland at a Hymn Festival in Lancaster on 5 October 2011. Notice there is a slightly different arrangement for verse 4 to accommodate the words. The tune, now named WINDRUSH, is frequently sung at Lancaster URC.

57. Millions of migrants, on the run

8.6.8.6.8.6   Based on Psalm 114

1. Millions of migrants, on the run
from Pharaoh's searing rod,
were heading for their future home—
the promised land of God,
whose ever-patient love and power
sustained them as they trod.

2. Waves of the sea recoiled and let
the refugees go by,
the river Jordan where they crossed
drew back to keep them dry,
while hills like startled animals
were seen to shake and shy.

3. Why does all nature quail before
events till now unknown?
Our God is sovereign in his world—
come bow to him alone
as pools appear in solid rock
and fountains flow from stone!

Emma Turl

Many of Emma Turl's hymns are based on Psalms or other scripture passages. The arresting first line of this hymn brings the Psalm directly into the present time. The image of migrants on the run is tragically familiar in our own day. Like God's People fleeing tyranny in Egypt, today's migrants have to face perilous seas and mountain crossings. Today's miracle would be for the landscape of prejudice and terror to quail before God's justice, as in the Psalm.

    Hymn texts (and tunes) continue to evolve over time, and Emma Turl continues to work on this text. If you are interested in joining that conversation, please contact the author via this book's website (see page iii).

58. Must we starve our children to pay our debts?

Maggie Hamilton

Towards the end of the last millennium, there was a campaign for the cancellation of Third World Debt by the year 2000. The campaign was organized by Jubilee 2000, under the slogan "Drop the Debt", and quickly caught the public imagination. Thousands of us headed up to Birmingham for the 1998 G8 Summit, to "Make a Chain to Break the Chains of Debt". We formed a human chain around the centre of the city, and, on a given signal, banged drums, yelled, sang, and generally raised a commotion to reach the ears of the decision-makers and opinion formers. Maggie Hamilton's song was written for that occasion. The first line is a direct quotation from Julius Nyerere, former President of Tanzania. Our commotion that day may not have physically reached the ears of the powerful, but the campaign had significant impact on British and global policies on global debt and development at the Millennium and in subsequent years.

Shout Jubilee

Composed for Make a Chain to Break the Chains of Debt event at the Birmingham G8 Summit

1. "Must we starve our children to pay our debts?"
Must we starve our children to pay our debts?
Must we starve our children to pay our debts?
How long must this go on?

Shout Jubilee! Set people free!
Break all the chains of debt!
Shout Jubilee! Set people free!
Break all the chains of debt!

2. "It's one law for the rich and another for the poor."
Shout Jubilee! …

3. "Debt destroys our families and our way of life."
Shout Jubilee! …

4. "We defend our roots as our country's base for growth."
Shout Jubilee! …

5. "Debt tears down our clinics and schools just as in war."
Shout Jubilee! …

6. "Now external debt has become eternal debt."
Shout Jubilee! …

7. People say, "One does not owe what one cannot pay."
Shout Jubilee! …

Maggie Hamilton

59. My God is beyond all imagining

My God is beyond all imagining
all pictures shatter, all word games empty
she is beyond, beneath, within, above
      the greatest mountains,
stars jewel in her fingers—
scattered with loving carelessness,
galaxies drift at her gaze
spiralling at her breath.

    She is   the pause before conception
               before the earth was born
               the flash of synapse as man drew breath.
    She is   the infinite dark that cradles us to birth
               the wait, the not-knowing.
    She is   the light that gives vision
               direction, hidden way, knowledge,
               healing, growth to new life.
    She is   beyond me and within me and around me.

    For her I was made, and there is no life without her.
    She held me when I would not be held
    and loved me when I would not be loved,
    directed my steps and guided my dreams
    cradled me in her arms when I was alone.

        She begins and ends my days, and with her
        I am shocked and loved and stunned at her grace.
        She begins and ends my days and without her
        there is no peace.
        She begins and ends my days
        and I am held in thrall.

        Praise her.

Wendy White

This gorgeous text is one of a set of poems by Wendy White, published in the first of a set of *Worship Live* issues focusing on the Trinity. The author draws from her own deep spirituality. As she is in God's image, she finds the wealth and intimacy of her own female experience reflected in the God she praises.

60. My mother—she was lovely!

Out of the mouths of babes: Bathsheba's little boy

See 2 Samuel 11–12, especially 12:15–25; Psalm 51 (including its heading); Matthew 1:1 and 6; also Isaiah 53:4; Matthew 10:29–30; 1 Peter 2:24.

My mother—she was lovely!
My father was the king;
my brother, wise and wealthy,
with many songs to sing.
I never knew my brother;
I died before he came;
my family is famous—
but no-one knows *my* name.

My parents were not married
the night I was conceived;
at least, not to each other,
if books may be believed.
I am—the son of David!
—the shepherd, king . . . and thief,
adulterer and killer,
who gave me life, and grief.

When Nathan told his story,
his parable of crime,
my father first was furious,
then silenced—for a time.
Then he was broken-hearted
and overcome with shame;
the prophet spoke his pardon
but—who will get the blame?

I may have lived—a fortnight?
Seven days of health and joy,
and seven of mystery illness—
a tiny, sickly boy.
My father wept and pleaded
with all a father's care;
for me he prayed and fasted,
but God . . . refused his prayer!

So I have borne his sorrows;
I had my Passion Week;
for God pronounced his judgement
before I learned to speak.
It fell on my small shoulders
before I had a voice,
I was a frail sin-bearer;
I did not have much choice.

And was it God who made me
then choked away my breath?
My parents held me, kissed me,
God gave—the kiss of death!
Another "Son of David"
called little ones his own;
he said, not even sparrows
fall to the ground alone.

I never ruled a nation
or led my troops to war,
or slaughtered tens of thousands
and longed to conquer more.
All that, and years of battles,
God spared me, by his grace;
instead, an infant coffin,
a prince's resting place.

Two chapters tell my story,
one penitential Psalm;
my father was forgiven,
and I sustained the harm.
But when I died, he worshipped,
from guilt and tears set free;
I never ran to meet him,
but he has come to me.

They often turn these pages
and fill the details in,
of lust and greed and murder
and lurid scenes of sin.
They struggle with the problem:
how could my father be
a man beloved by heaven?
They do not mention me!

My mother, twice a widow,
she reached a ripe old age.
She saw her son (my brother)
take over centre stage.
My mother—she was lovely;
from her I drew my life,
her name is not forgotten;
she was—Uriah's wife.

Christopher Idle

Christopher Idle is well known as a writer of hymns that challenge and delight, and one of the architects of the Hymn Explosion as a writer and involved in the compilation of hymn resources. In this poem, he shines a light on a well-known story from an almost unknown standpoint. The result of David's murderous adultery with Bathsheba was not Solomon, as is often thought. There was another child, whose story is never told. Idle allows him a voice, and the familiar narrative, with its messianic overtones, takes a different shape.

61. No height so high, no depth so low

Gill Gilbert

KINGSLEY

8.8.8.8.8.8

No height so high, no depth so low,
no force of nature so extreme,
no human law, no earthly power,
no fearful fantasy or dream
can tear us from the love of Christ.
For this his life was sacrificed.

Jenny Wakely

Words © Jenny Wakely/Jubilate Hymns. Administered by The Jubilate Group, Kitley House, St Katherines Road, Torquay TQ1 4DE, copyrightmanager@jubilate.co.uk.

This one-verse text based on verses from Romans 8:38–39 appeared in an issue of *Worship Live* (no. 51) focusing on starting points in worship. The editorial comment notes that worship begins with a sense of entering into God's presence, and the simple power of these words reminds us of the love of God in Christ, always open to us.

62. O God, by whom our yesterdays

Ian Sharp

ALDWICK GRANGE

O God, by whom our yesterdays are known and valued still, we here entrust our future ways to your creative will.

Both Elizabeth Cosnett and Ian Sharp are established hymnists, and Ian has written several tunes to Elizabeth's texts.

Elizabeth writes:

> This hymn was written for the installation of Nicholas Frayling as Dean of Chichester and would be appropriate for other situations involving new beginnings. It refers to the legend of the overturned chalice, which is often shown in images or statues of St Richard of Chichester and appears in one of his coats of arms. The story is that St Richard was celebrating mass while tired from his labours, and dropped the chalice with the consecrated wine, taken to be the very blood of Christ. When the chalice was taken up again, it was found that, miraculously, none of the wine had been spilt.

CM

1. O God, by whom our yesterdays
are known and valued still,
we here entrust our future ways
to your creative will.

2. Here saints have worshipped, laughed and cried,
have shared each day the cup
of one who suffered, failed and died,
whom you have lifted up.

3. Now comes our turn to take the stage,
a chance to witness here,
in this, our place, and this, our age,
to all he holds most dear.

4. And shall we leave him in the lurch,
in all our neighbours found?
Make us an outward looking church,
a chalice handed round.

5. Let thus the precious blood of Christ
become our lifeblood too,
and we, both saved and sacrificed,
a sign that points to you.

Elizabeth Cosnett

Words and Music © Copyright 2003 Stainer & Bell Ltd. Reprinted by permission.

63. Oh my Spirit will flow like the river of life

Jeanne Blowers

The third of the series of issues on the Trinity focuses on the Spirit of God. Jeanne Blowers' hymn explores the image of the Spirit as the river of life, flowing through the heart of the heavenly city, as described in the eschatological vision in the book of Revelation.

For the Healing of Nations
Irreg.

Oh my Spirit will flow like the river of life
and my love will grow like a tree
and the leaves of that tree in the hands of my loved
for the healing of nations will be.

1. For I am your God
and my love will reign for evermore,
for I am your God
and my Lamb will set you free.
Chorus

2. And night will be no more
and you'll need no light from lamp or sun
and night will be no more
for I will be your light.
Chorus

Jeanne Blowers

64. O sun of Wisdom, arise

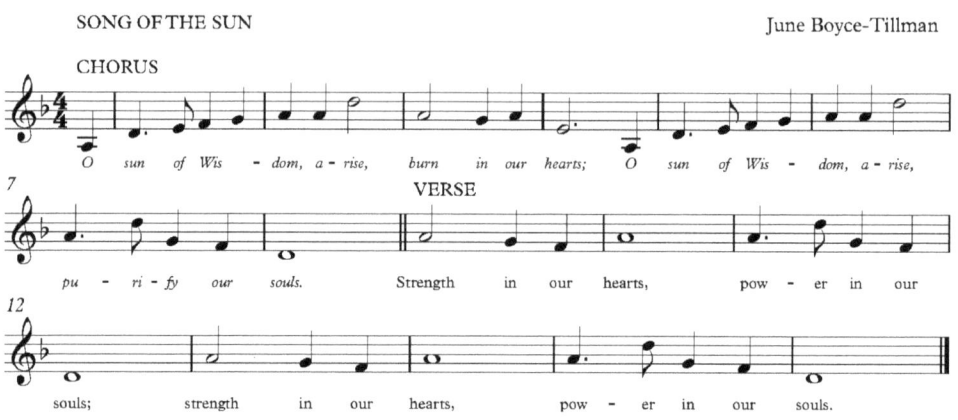

SONG OF THE SUN — June Boyce-Tillman

CHORUS: O sun of Wisdom, arise, burn in our hearts; O sun of Wisdom, arise, purify our souls.

VERSE: Strength in our hearts, power in our souls; strength in our hearts, power in our souls.

June Boyce-Tillman is a prolific writer, composer and musicologist. She was involved in compiling a number of hymn resources published by Galliard in the 1970s, including *New Orbit* (1972) and *New Horizons* (1974). Since then, she has written widely on music, spirituality, healing and wholeness. She is a keen advocate of inclusive language in hymns, and also positive female language in singing of God and the created world. This simple text was published in the second of a series of issues on the Trinity. It is a hymn to Wisdom, who is, of course, a female figure in scripture.

Song of the Sun

O sun of Wisdom, arise,
burn in our hearts;
O sun of Wisdom, arise,
purify our souls.

1. Strength in our hearts,
power in our souls;
strength in our hearts,
power in our souls.
Chorus

2. Warmth in our hearts,
loving in our souls;
warmth in our hearts,
loving in our souls.
Chorus

3. Flame in our hearts,
peace within our souls;
flame in our hearts,
peace within our souls.
Chorus

June Boyce-Tillman

Words and Music © Copyright 2006 Stainer & Bell Ltd. Reprinted by permission.

65. Oh the bliss of a bit of shelter

Expectation—A meditation
Oh the bliss of a bit of shelter,
some straw to lie down on
after that interminable journey;
somewhere to rest between pains.
I thought we'd never make it
at one stage—the checkpoint
as we entered Bethlehem.
Thank God for a compassionate soldier,
and the kindly innkeeper—
she obviously understood
what I was going through.

Here in the quiet, away from the crowds,
surrounded by the warmth of animals
and the solicitous strength of Joseph,
I can get on with things.
I never imagined when I agreed
to Gabriel's request from God
that it was going to be like this.
I didn't expect a palace
but hoped for a home and maybe
my mother and the local midwife
to help out, or even cousin Elisabeth—
she's been through it recently.

The trouble is, when you say "Yes" to God,
you never know what to expect!

Carol Dixon

We have published a number of hymns by Carol Dixon over the years, and are thrilled to see that some of her texts have recently found a place in *Church Hymnary 4th edition* (2005). This meditation on the birth of Jesus looks at the event from the standpoint of Mary, forced to travel away from home just as the birth falls due. The checkpoint and the soldier remind us that this is still divided and disputed territory. And in our time, when so many are driven from their homes, the longing for the familiar support of family and community for a birth strikes all too true a note.

66. On Calvary, life's light

6.4.6.4D

1. On Calvary, life's light
was found too frail,
a candle in the night
against death's gale;
yet in its dying flame
resplendent grace
outshines all human shame,
from that dark place.

2. And now, when death's wind blows,
the flame is fanned,
and as its brightness grows
we understand:
the candle's faintest glow
has filled death's night
and in its flame we know
eternal light.

3. The brightness of the sun
is dark beside
the resurrected One
whose flame once died;
and with enlightened eyes,
when death is past,
in Christ we recognize
ourselves at last!

4. His mirror-light reveals
us as we are,
his image in us heals
each stain and scar,
and, on the Wind, we ride
so free and wild,
each one identified
–God's dazzling child!

Alan Gaunt

Words © Copyright 2000 Stainer & Bell Ltd. Reprinted by permission.

The third issue in the series on the Trinity included a number of hymns and other items tracing the presence of the Spirit of God through the life, death and resurrection of Jesus. The editorial note records that "the same Spirit that drove Jesus into the wilderness came upon the disciples at Pentecost". Alan Gaunt's text brilliantly interweaves God's image (mirror-like), with flame, light and wind, in dense, rich language, which will grow in the singing. The hymn appears in his collection *Delight that Never Dies* (2003), set to a new tune, HAYMARKET, by Paul Bateman. Gaunt notes that it arises out of Wallace Stevens' poem "Valley Candle".

67. Our wonder grows and deepens with the years

Our wonder grows and deepens with the years,
we hear more in what people write and say.
Piece by small piece a unity appears.

The breezes blow, the misty morning clears,
changes in light give meaning to the day.
Our wonder grows and deepens with the years.

Youth is a phase of laughter and of tears,
for lessons learned there is a price to pay.
Piece by small piece a unity appears.

In middle years come questionings and fears;
the disillusioned heart is apt to stray
but wonder grows and deepens with the years.

Tranquillity—the treasure age reveres
is found along a narrow, twisting way.
Piece by small piece a unity appears.

The troubles which assail, the pain which sears
transform the heart to gold or else to clay.
Our wonder grows and deepens with the years
as piece by piece a unity appears.

John Adamson Brown

We published a number of John Adamson Brown's poems in *Worship Live*. All are carefully constructed and rich in texture. This text appeared in an issue focusing on diversity and unity, which contained a lot of material about diverse communities. But there is also a movement between diversity and unity in each human life, a process of change, which the first line describes dynamically: "Our wonder grows and deepens with the years." This line recurs through the poem in counterpoint with the experience that unity appears "piece by small piece". In the process of editing this book, I have come back to this poem 20 years after first preparing it for publication. I find that I have genuinely moved through the verses, and find the whole piece still, and newly, true to my own experience.

68. Present at the world's creation

8.4.8.4.8.8.8.4   Suggested tunes: EAST ACKLAM or AR HYD Y NOS

1. Present at the world's creation,
Spirit of God;
summoning a chosen nation,
Spirit of God;
swift to guide and to deliver
through the wilderness and river;
sanctifying Lord, life-giver,
Spirit of God.

2. Yours a power beyond all measure;
we worship you.
Source of courage, wisdom's treasure:
we worship you.
Lord, inspiring prophets' vision,
overcoming all division;
Lord who calls us to decision,
we worship you.

3. Spirit, by your proclamation
all now are one.
Culture, status, generation—
all now are one.
Every tribe and tongue addressing,
truth of Jesus Christ confessing,
turning Babel into blessing:
all now are one.

4. Seeds for future harvest sowing,
speak to us now.
Gifts revealing, grace bestowing,
speak to us now.
You have shaped our past tradition,
you restore and recondition;
fit us now for our commission:
speak to us now!

Dominic Grant

The feast of Pentecost opens the way for a far broader exploration of the Holy Spirit than simply the story in the book of Acts. The Spirit of God is a force throughout scripture, from Genesis to Revelation, as recognized in Dominic Grant's text. The first three verses celebrate the acts of the Spirit, culminating in the final verse, in which the congregation enters into the experience: "Speak to us now."

69. Ruth, don't do it

Advice
Ruth, don't do it. You don't know
what you're promising.
Your people will be my people,
your God will be my God—
but Ruth, that will never happen.

You will be severed from your roots,
a tree trunk chopped down, cast to drift
in foreign waters. You can never
grow new roots.

You will lose your family, those
who love you, speak your language,
share your history.

These people will try, but they can't
use your words, know your heart.
You will always be *that Moabite girl.*

You will not be present at your mother's
departure. You will know your sisters
only in memory glimpses. There will be
no-one to giggle with late at night.

So Ruth, don't do it. Don't go
to your husband's people—
he is dead, let his memory
be enough.

Stay with your own.
Be secure, understood
and unfulfilled.

Kaye Lee

We published several poems and reflections by Kaye Lee during the lifetime of *Worship Live*. She would often bring fresh insights to well-known biblical narratives, as here, approaching the life story of Ruth from the point of view of "advisers" from among her own people. In an era, such as ours, when so many people face terrible decisions about staying in familiar but difficult circumstances, or relocating to seek a new life, Kaye reflects the nuances of loss and alienation involved in such choices. The punch line, in the case of Ruth, lies in the very last word of the poem. If she remains, lives among her own, she will be forever "unfulfilled".

70. See he comes in modest manner

8.7.8.7.8.7   Suggested tune: ST HELEN

1. See he comes in modest manner;
King of Kings and Lord of Lords,
yet he rides upon a donkey,
crowds wave palms instead of swords.
Sing hosanna! Sing hosanna
to the King and Lord of Lords.

2. See his anger in the Temple,
fixing traders with a glare,
so he overthrows their tables
in his Father's house of prayer.
Sing hosanna! Sing hosanna
to the King who's always there.

3. See him leave the Temple precinct
as he prays for strength and grace
that his soul would meet the challenge
of the cross he has to face.
Sing hosanna! Sing hosanna
to the King who takes our place.

Hugh Naunton

Hugh Naunton was a regular participant in our writing weekends, and we were pleased to publish a number of his hymns.

This text was written at the 2004 weekend, held over Palm Sunday weekend at Holland House, Cropthorne. Carolyn Sanderson, who organized this weekend with her husband, Mike, said: "Group members commented appreciatively on the inspiration and encouragement they received from each other, and all enjoyed the warm sense of fellowship that developed remarkably quickly." Since publication in *Worship Live*, Hugh has added a further two verses, between vss 1 and 2, which can be found on HymnQuest.

71. She threw the bucket down the well

At the Well
She threw the bucket down the well
drew her water abandoned
caring not for your thoughts
she was mistress of herself,
and it threw you,
it was new to you,
her strength and sure ways
her head high and proud,
you vulnerable, and in need,
would she give you,
this was her chance
like never before,
in command,
she had power
to withhold
she enjoyed it,
the freedom
the choosing
you gave her,
she forgave you
and you thirsted no more.

Patricia Randall

Patricia Randall was a regular contributor to *Worship Live* over the years. Her poems were perceptive, and often challenging. Here, she takes seriously the approach of Jesus to the woman at the well. In something of a turning of tables, he asks her for water. The poem follows this thought through the whole extraordinary encounter, to startling effect.

72. Sing praise for Hebrew midwives

7.6.7.6D   Suggested tune: MERLE'S TUNE

1. Sing praise for Hebrew midwives,
they bravely served their God;
they brought to birth God's people,
a remnant was preserved.
They used both fact and fiction,
and found a cunning way
to counter male dominion,
and give God's will full sway.

2. Praise, too, the loving mother
who saved her son from death.
She placed him in the water
with trembling, fearful breath.
Then Pharaoh's daughter entered,
and found the hidden one.
Defying her own father,
she took him for her son.

3. Sing praise for this son, Moses,
who, by the midwives' act,
was saved to lead God's people,
and given faith he lacked.
Revere defiant women
who seek to bring to birth
new life from wombs of darkness
to live God's will on earth.

Edith Sinclair Downing

© Wayne Leupold Editions Inc. The Leupold Foundation, 8510 Triad Drive, Colfax, NC 27235, USA., contact@theleupoldfoundation.org. www.theleupoldfoundation.org

The summer 2007 issue of *Worship Live* (no. 38) commemorated the bicentenary of the ending of the transatlantic trade in enslaved people in 1807. The editorial note (slightly amended) read:

> The songs of the people enslaved and forced to work on plantations in America and the Caribbean in the eighteenth and nineteenth centuries were steeped in the scriptures. The Bible is a dangerous instrument to put into people's hands, and the story and theology of the Exodus soon focused both the injustice of slavery and the divine promise of freedom. Edith Sinclair Downing here reminds us that the Exodus depended not just on Moses' reluctant obedience to God's call, but also on the courage and ingenuity of the women who resisted the barbaric cruelties of the slave-owners of their own time.

73. Soaked by the spray from these turbulent waters

Isles of the North Rejoice

11.10.11.11.10.10.11.10   Suggested tune: DA ISLES OF GLETNESS

1. Soaked by the spray from these turbulent waters,
swept by long gales through the short hours of day,
sun-glistened seabirds, resplendent and raucous,
sing, as God's light sheds his glory in grey:
lands of rich music, dancing in firelight,
tunes of today merge with tales of the past;
isles of the north, sing your songs of rejoicing,
led by God's love from the first to the last.

2. Blyde* to forgather in faith and in friendship,
blyde to be here in this breathtaking place,
blest as we celebrate beauty in smallness,
scattered, united, refreshed by God's grace;
buoyed by our part in serving Christ's kingdom,
gifts are discerned as we fervently pray;
isles of the north sing your songs of rejoicing,
called and confirmed by the Christ of today.

3. Joined by our Network of witness and service,
boldly *encouraging* unexplored ways,
filled by the life-giving Spirit's resources,
daily *equipping* our prayer and our praise;
fired by the call to be Christ's disciples,
humbly *enabling* the gifts each one shares;
isles of the north sing your songs of rejoicing,
drawn by the Spirit who drives and who dares.

4. God, when we flounder in rudderless drifting,
you are our Rock in the wild surging sea;
you are the wind that whips all our pretences
into the truth that will set us all free;
you are the calm deep place of our praying,
you are the strength of each wavering voice,
thankful today, we embark on our future,
isles of the north with God's people rejoice.

Tom Wilkinson

*Blyde is an original Shetland word, meaning "glad".

The author writes:

> This hymn was written for a Regional Gathering of five Methodist Districts—Darlington, Newcastle, Cumbria, Scotland and Shetland—and took place 1–4 June 2007. The event was organized by the Women's Network Committee of each of these Districts, and it was their first gathering in Shetland. I was asked to write a suitable text. The italic words in verse three —encouraging, equipping, enabling—are featured on the logo of Women's Network. The tune is a Shetland Song called 'Da Isles of Gletness', written many years ago by a local man, John T. Barclay, now deceased.

As it happens, the event was recalled in the Shetland Methodist Church's magazine, *Contact*, which coincidentally appeared as this book was going to press. This notes that the weekend of celebrations included: "Praise Services in Lerwick, Haroldswick and Walls . . . a pilgrimage and communion on St. Ninian's Isle." One attendee commented: "Never have I felt so blessed by a Conference or so deeply aware of the spirituality of [these] islands."

74. The holiness of God is veiled

HOLY WELL
Trad - arranged by Nicholas Williams

Arrangement © Copyright Stainer & Bell Ltd. Reprinted by permission.

8.6.8.6D

1. The holiness of God is veiled
from all but God alone,
and those who seek can only find
a God, as yet unknown,
who leads us on life's narrow paths,
walks with us hand in hand
and gives us insight into truths
we do not understand.

2. God cries to us in wind and storm
and whispers in the calm,
"I'll lift you up on eagles' wings
and hold you in my palm.
I am the God of rich and poor,
of every race and creed.
I know each longing, hope and fear,
and feel your deepest need."

3. Beyond the reach of eyes and ears,
yet standing close beside;
we look and cannot see the God
who is our friend and guide.
We listen and we do not hear
the words of truth and grace,
but then we turn and feel a breath
blow gently on our face.

4. Our intellect may seek for ways
to limit and explain
the complex deity of God
which words cannot contain;
but faith alone can comprehend
the deepest mystery
and know that God is here on earth,
yet reigns in majesty.

Moira Rose

At the turn of the Millennium, Worship Live ran a competition for hymns and songs on the theme of "The Dawning of a New Age". Of around 100 entries, a good number were of really high quality. The judges selected two winners: one "hymn" and one "song". These were sung at the conference, Singing in the New Millennium in October 2000 (see Preface), and published in Worship Live issue 19 in spring 2001.

Moira Rose's hymn is set to a traditional tune, HOLY WELL, arranged by Nicholas Williams. The winner in the song category can be found in the same issue of Worship Live: "Walking to a grave, filled with dread", words and music by Tony Ingleby.

75. The soldiers by and large were decent men

Disadvantage

10.10.10.10D

1. The soldiers by and large were decent men
but overtaken by an evil day.
Perhaps they really thought the kid was armed,
perhaps the woman just got in the way.
Perhaps they were frustrated and abused
and so remembered what their guns were for.
The soldiers by and large were decent men
but that's a disadvantage in a war.

2. The citizens were civilized enough
but overwhelmed by suffering too great,
with homes and friends and children all destroyed
by infidels who claimed to liberate.
Why should they not be seized with righteous rage
and take some lives to even up the score?
The citizens were civilized enough
but that's a disadvantage in a war.

3. The leader always meant to tell the truth,
believing in the rightness of his cause,
but people seemed reluctant to be led
and kept appealing to obstructive laws.
It wasn't that he peddled blatant lies,
just stretched the truth to mean a little more.
The leader always meant to tell the truth
but that's a disadvantage in a war.

4. And would they recognize the man who stood,
not armed, not hostile, violent or proud,
and challenged them with love to love the good,
the leader and the soldiers and the crowd?
And would they nail his body to a tree
for reasons they could blame upon the strife,
or turn away from killing and be free?
For war's a disadvantage in a life.

Sue Gilmurray

It was wonderful to have Sue Gilmurray at our writing weekends. She brought fresh insight to the writing of texts, and also the gift of composing music and advising on the use of tunes. In *This is our Song* (2010, p. 287), she writes: "I have never thought of myself primarily as a hymn writer . . . When, for the first time, I joined others on a hymn writing weekend in the autumn of 2008, I felt quite at home: the territory was familiar. Much of my creative output, however, refuses to fit neatly into the 'hymn' category."

This is true of this deeply thoughtful text and tune, about which she writes: "I'll never forget how it came together, after reading an article by Robert Fisk about the town of Fallujah after the British Invasion of Iraq: writing of how the soldiers were doing their best, and the Iraqi people were wondering whether to rebel, and Tony Blair thought he wasn't bending the facts too much—and how with the invading army, the resentful people of another faith, and a leader who was ambivalent about the truth, I had assembled all the cast of the story of Jesus' passion except for Jesus." (email, 24 December 2022)

76. These are the hands

These are the hands
These are the hands that have done so much harm,
starting battles and wars, for people, once calm.
These are the hands that hold onto the gun,
a pull of the trigger and death has been done.

These are the hands that made a great bomb,
killing more people than died at the Somme.
These are the hands that fly the great plane,
dropping bombs over cities, it's all so insane!

These are the hands which wipe away tears,
of people so sad, with so many fears.
These are the hands, waving farewell,
to millions of soldiers, who face living hell.

These are the hands, which comfort the lame,
bruised, broken bodies, it's all such a shame.
These are the hands which bury the mine,
causing havoc and death on the enemy line.

These are the hands, trying so hard to repair,
broken up families, it's all so unfair!
These are the hands which hide faces in shame,
when children are orphaned, who takes the blame?

These are the hands joined together in prayer,
remembering the dead, to show that we care.
These are the hands which join together to pray,
that wars will be history; that'll be the day!

These are the hands that release the white dove,
sending peace to our world, which all of us love.

Written by Year 5 pupils of The Paragon School, Bath

Class teacher, Mr Chris Guest, commented:

> Several years ago, a Year 5 class at The Paragon School wrote a poem called, "These are the Hands" for their Remembrance assembly.
>
> Last November, some of the present Year 5 pupils performed the same poem for the "Bath and District Poppy Appeal Launch". Many people spectating, including the Mayor of Bath and members of the British Legion, were so impressed by the children's performance, that an invitation was offered to perform the poem at a World War I Centenary Celebration in Bath Abbey. The children surpassed themselves, giving a moving tribute to our fallen ancestors.

We were delighted to include several collaborative texts like this. See, for example, no. 6, 83.

77. To pray is to extol

Neville Favell

AVON MEADOWS

A Hymn in Acknowledgment of Prayer

6.6.6.6.4.4.4.4

1. To pray is to extol
God's power divine; love's grace
conferred on humble hearts—
this trembling human race!
    In silent awe
    or vibrant bliss,
    high purpose this,
    his gaze to bear!

2. To pray is gratitude:
God's gracious name be blessed!
Good providence reviewed
prompts boundless thanks expressed:
    love deep, divine,
    stir hearts ablaze:
    let rapturous praise
    our souls invest!

3. To pray is to confess;
fault, failure, grievous shame:
offence, remorse, regret,
admission of deep blame!
    Yet, full assured
    Christ crucified,
    who for us died,
    all shall reclaim!

4. To pray is to entreat
the enlightening Spirit's beam
be shed upon the pilgrim's way;
each step redeem!
    To love respond:
    Christ's powers embrace,
    his path retrace,
    his truths esteem!

5. To pray is to explore
God's plan for humankind:
to crave his care to compass
all we bring to mind:
    stranger or friend;
    their ills to mend,
    their strengths defend;
    by Christ designed!

6. To pray is to revere;
make reckoning of God's grace:
uplifting heart and voice
with rapturous, radiant face!
    Almighty love,
    creator, friend,
    beginning, end!
    Ours to embrace!

Neville Ashton

This hymn and tune found their place in an issue of *Worship Live* (no. 25) on the theme of prayer. The editorial recalls lines from a hymn by James Montgomery: "Prayer is the Christian's vital breath / the Christian's native air", noting that Montgomery was a controversial writer, and activist in social causes: "The writer who describes prayer as the Christian's vital breath is no quiet contemplative." Neville Ashton's hymn explores the range of prayer in the Christian life, from awe and bliss, through thankfulness and confession, and active care, to return to the rapturous embrace of God's love. Neville Favell's lyrical tune allows space for the intensity of the words to reach into the hearts of worshippers.

78. Tread softly

Tread Softly in the Close

Tread softly:

The spider,
watchman of the cathedral close,
alert arachnid
ominously hunched up,
poised tight in its portal web,
spins silky strands of death beneath weathered gargoyles.

Tread softly:

The snail,
shell-encumbered gastropod of night,
probes,
tentacles testing the cloisters' dank air,
then thrusts forward supple on softly muscled foot,
its glistening trail of slime etching the damp flags.

Tread softly:

The toad,
poisonous reptilian,
darkly bloated,
squat in its blunt obesity,
crouches in the shadow of the chapel wall,
shed skin dangling dryly from its warty lips.

Tread softly in the close
as you cross to light candles
on the high altar;
for I am there:
in the spider,
the snail,
and the toad,
not just in the works of man.

Turn a stone, I am there;
crack a shell, I am there;
dig a pit, I am there.

I am the Lord.

John Helliwell

We were pleased to publish a number of items by John Helliwell during the lifetime of *Worship Live*. Always thoughtful, John's poems often reached beyond the usual perception of biblical events, or the world we live in. This poem appeared in the first of a series of issues on the Trinity, in which, the editorial notes, there was "a lot of fun with creation, as there is in the Bible—enjoying the strangeness and complexity of the world we share [with nature]". This intense text reminds us that we meet God in the creatures that inhabit the Cathedral Close, as much as at the high altar within.

79. Tree of wisdom, give us shelter

She is the tree of life
Inspired by Proverbs 3:18 "She is a tree of life to those who lay hold of her; those who hold her fast are called happy."

8.7.8.7 Trochaic   Suggested tune: SERVANT SONG

1. Tree of wisdom, give us shelter,
shade beneath your branches wide,
tree of life as God our maker,
comforted at Jesus' side.

2. Branches reaching out in wonder,
tree of life with such strong frame.
Help us cast our pains asunder,
claim our lives in your sweet name.

3. Springtime's days with such fresh promise
daring buds to quest and grow.
Resurrect our sense of homage,
shoots of green from what you sow.

4. Canopy of radiant splendour,
blossom, fruit and leaves and birds.
Fullest shape of greening wonder,
tree of life, we love your Word.

5. All the colours of sweet autumn
show us hues of Godly change.
Help us greet this phase of waiting,
we are yours to rearrange.

6. When we see great change before us,
challenges we must endure.
Give us roots in your deep wisdom
help us, God, to be secure.

7. Glimpsing heaven through the treetops;
canopy of love and space.
Help us build your wisdom earthwards,
golden leaves of peace and grace.

Sara Iles

Our 2015 writers' weekend, at the Windermere Centre, was on the theme of healing. The editorial notes: "Although there was some focus on the pain that so often precedes healing, we discovered that wonderment and amazement are never far behind, as explored by Sara Iles, who was attending the hymn writing weekend for the first time." The verses trace the life of the tree through the seasons, deftly weaving the pattern of natural change into the texture of human life, shaped by wisdom. Since writing this hymn, Sara has gone on to encourage others, through, for example, setting up a team to run hymn writing workshops in the Congregational Federation.

80. We celebrate God's word to us

8.7.8.7.8.8.7   Suggested tune: MIT FREUDEN ZART

1. We celebrate God's word to us,
our living inspiration,
passed on and treasured for its truth
through every generation.
Though values change, God's word remains
our source of hope that strengthens us,
and draws us closer to him.

2. Deep woven through each Bible page
in vibrant song and story,
the ancient memories are entwined
that speak of God's great glory.
Through prophecy and history,
in sad lament and joyful praise,
runs faith that spans the ages.

3. God's love transcends the turning years,
in glorious revelation;
through God in Christ, the Word made flesh,
the promise of salvation.
By day and night, by candlelight,
by word of mouth and sweep of pen,
these truths have been recorded.

Jan Grimwood

Occasionally, issues of *Worship Live* focused on various points in the act of worship itself. In the autumn of 2011 (Issue 51), we looked at starting points in worship. Jan Grimwood's hymn, set to the lovely German tune MIT FREUDEN ZART, sets the reading of scripture at the heart of worship. Typography is important: the "word" in scripture culminates in the "Word" made flesh, and the hymn ends with a beautiful visual image of the transmission of the story of salvation which brings us to the point where, in an act of worship, we now encounter word, and Word.

81. We happily could spend our days

Healing the Church

LM Suggested tune: WINCHESTER NEW

1. We happily could spend our days
in singing God great hymns of praise.
But what we really ought to give
is praising in the way we live.

2. "Made in God's image"—get it right!
"Live in the light, for God is light."
John's teaching comes from heaven above:
"Love one another, God is love."

3. It seems straightforward, yet we know
the world's sunk to an all-time low!
The Church, too often, struggles too;
let down by folks like us, that's true!

4. Lord, lay on us your healing hand
and, as your Church, we'll gladly stand:
with wholeness and in harmony
we'll live life as it's meant to be.

David Lemmon

David Lemmon was a regular participant at our writing weekends, and this hymn was written at the 2015 weekend at the Windermere Centre. The theme was Healing and David's text invites us to consider that the Church itself stands in dire need of God's healing touch. The words are straightforward and challenging.

82. We know the songs of Zion from our youth

Copyright © 1993 Stainer and Bell

In Exile

10.10.8.4.8.7.9.12   Based on Psalm 137

1. We know the songs of Zion from our youth,
but who can make us sing them, speak their truth
and compel from us their secret
in a strange land?
By the rivers of Babylon, we listen and remember.
We hang our harps on the willow tree
And the music of our grief is in the silence.

2. Our children marry as the years slip by.
We must not let the songs of Zion die,
nor trust others with their secret
in a strange land.
Chorus

3. If we forget our roots and destiny,
we lose our faith in our identity,
so our language is our secret
in a strange land.
Chorus

4. Our preservation and integrity
must be maintained through our captivity,
and so strictures guard our secret
in a strange land.
Chorus

5. The threat of being absorbed fills us with fear:
we must be seen and heard or disappear,
for they hold us with our secret
in a strange land.
Chorus

Lois Ainger

Words and Music © Copyright 1993 Stainer & Bell Ltd. Reprinted by permission.

I first came across Lois Ainger's hymns when working with June Boyce-Tillman on *Reflecting Praise* (1993), in which we included a number of her hymns. She has also been a regular contributor to *Worship Live*, and to a number of other Stainer & Bell publications: *Story Song* (1993) and *Sound Bytes* (1999) among them. This dramatic and powerful song erupts into movement from the first line of words and music. It is based on the Psalm of exile, Psalm 137, and draws out the bitter isolation of that experience, the more powerfully because it is based on the author's own experience of evacuation from occupied Guernsey, in the Channel Islands, during the Second World War. In an age when more and more people are driven into exile or flight, the words must ring true to many.

83. WE LOVE

Marlene Phillips

Yealand Harvest Song

Irregular

1. WE LOVE:
ripe, red raspberries, lemons so tart,
dark green cabbage with a crisp, crunchy heart,
orange carrots in a deep garden bed,
wheat for flour to make into bread.
Thank you Father for the sun and the rain
to ripen our vegetables, fruit and grain.

2. WE LOVE:
fine, fat gooseberries, covered with hairs,
tangy oranges and sweet, speckled pears,
plums and damsons, hanging low on the trees,
broad beans, flat beans, pod-popping peas.
Thank you Father for the sun and the rain
to ripen our vegetables, fruit and grain.

3. WE LOVE:
salt that's harvested from briny seas,
season's fish we enjoy for our teas,
milk from dairy cows and trout from the stream,
succulent strawberries, smothered in cream.
Thank you Father for the sun and the rain
to ripen our vegetables, fruit and grain.

4. WE KNOW:
countries where crops cannot grow;
no rain falls when only dry breezes blow;
burnt grass shrivels and the animals die;
children starve—much too weak to cry.
Show us, Father, how to ease their pain,
so they can learn to smile again.

5. THEY NEED:
wells for water and strong, sprouting seed
chickens, donkeys, goats and animal feed,
time for singing, dancing, learning and play
giving them a chance to say:
Thank you Father for the sun and the rain
to ripen our vegetables, fruit and grain.

Sheila Kelly and pupils of Yealand Primary School

Marlene Phillips, who composed the tune for this hymn, writes:

> At harvest time . . . Sheila and I were asked by the headmistress of the village school at Yealand in Lancashire to produce a harvest song by working with the children. I took along a few ideas and several sheets of paper, but Sheila toured the local supermarket and produced a large basket of fruit and vegetables of various colours, textures, smells and sizes. While Sheila talked about the content of each verse, I made mental notes about the rhythms of words and talked about the excitement of rhythm. There was no shortage of

ideas, not only about our own harvest, but about harvest time in drought-stricken countries.

Finding ourselves with many notes and scribblings after this first session, we tried to express the enthusiasm of the children and the wish to share and find solutions without the result being too naïve or too sophisticated. The music springs directly from the rhythms and pitch of the words, the many syllables to a line producing a sense of excitement.

I hope this effort will be followed by others. It would be good to have the children composing their very own tunes.

In fact, other similar collaborative items can be found at no. 6, 76.

Sheila's son, Graham Kelly, comments, about his mother: "Mum was always writing stuff—a LOT of poems for friends and relatives etc.... Rarely would a special occasion go by without us receiving her latest creation!" (email, 22 August 2022) It is a privilege to include this result of her talent in teaching and writing.

84. Weep with us for the islands

7.7.7.6.4.4.5.6   Suggested tune: PO KARE KARE

1. Weep with us for the islands—
jewels in a shining sea.
Peopled with long tradition
and strong community.
As the seas rise,
all we hold dear,
lands, story and lives
will simply disappear.

2. Speak with us to the powerful.
Tell them that we are here.
These oceans are not empty.
These islands live in fear.
Join our concern.
Our voice and yours
might make the world learn
to save a rich resource.

3. Weep with us for the forest.
Weep for the living wood
torn open by the chainsaws,
dead roots ploughed into mud.
While trees are burned,
clearings carved out,
all that we have earned
is lost in flood and drought.

4. Work with us in replanting.
Work with us to make good
olive and eucalyptus,
wildlife and living wood.
Join with our hands.
Touch the rich earth,
which simply demands
we recognize its worth.

Janet Wootton

Words © Copyright 2007 Stainer & Bell Ltd. Reprinted by permission.

In *Eagles' Wings* (2007), Janet Wootton writes:

> [T]his text was written at a conference of the Council for World Mission, following presentations by Pacific Islanders and the people of Madagascar about the issues confronting them. The Polynesian folk tune seemed appropriate to the theme. At the time (1990), the issue in the Pacific was nuclear testing ... Now (2007) the same islanders are seeing the rise in sea level threaten their very existence. Madagascar shares the problems of many forested areas (deforestation and destruction of habitat). Olive and eucalyptus are fast-growing trees which are planted to reclaim devastated areas of former forest.

The text was published in *Worship Live* in the summer of 1997, in an issue (no. 8) with a broad international focus. It appeared in *Eagles' Wings* (2007) with the altered first verse. This is the version which is now copyrighted by Stainer & Bell.

85. When mountains that we thought secure

CMD Suggested tune: VOX DILECTI

Written in response to 9/11

1. When mountains that we thought secure
lie crumbled where we stand
and pain and helplessness endure
—all from another's hand—
help us to bear the prophet's mark,
to stand apart from hate
and witness to the Father's call
for justice in the land.

2. God is our strength and refuge still
though all the earth give way;
our help at every time of ill,
the light of our dark day.
And as his people in the world
we bear the scars of grief,
but echo faith's resounding note
—and still for justice pray.

3. There is a place of holiness
where God makes warfare cease.
There is a day of hopefulness,
a promised time of peace.
So, here today, we bear the pain
of inhumanity,
but pledge our lives to live for truth
so justice may increase.

Gareth Hill

Unsurprisingly, the first decade of the new millennium saw a flow of material in to *Worship Live* responding to conflict in different parts of the world. This spurred the editors to focus an issue in 2009 on the theme of War and Peace including specific areas of conflict. The editorial speaks of a "longing for peace that is based on fairness" but also "a recognition of the wisdom and effort that is needed to unravel the tangle of injustice and hurt". Gareth Hill's text, written in response to 9/11, captures that moment of pain, helplessness and grief, but also commitment to pray for justice and live for truth. The tune VOX DILECTI, with its dramatic movement between the two halves of the verse, suits the words well. We were also delighted when one of our regular composers, Gwilym Beechey, wrote a new tune, JUSTICE, which appeared in summer 2010, an issue whose theme was Looking forward (no. 47).

86. When seen from vastnesses of space

Bill Chessum

Hazelnut
LM

1. When seen from vastnesses of space,
how beautiful—and yet how small—
appears the Earth, our dwelling place,
which struggles to sustain us all.

2. And, viewed from faith's immensity,
our fragile world—air, sea and land—
is loved with great intensity
and cradled in its Maker's hand.

3. May we, as if in orbit too,
the astronauts' pure wonder share,
and pledge ourselves to learn anew
for each created thing to care.

4. So shall we then by faith perceive—
with Julian in her Norwich cell—
and have the courage to believe
that all things truly shall be well.

Norman Goreham

The issue editor comments:

> Norman used the work of the mystic Mother Julian of Norwich (c.1342–1420) and her image of a hazelnut as his inspiration:
> "And in this he showed me something small, no bigger than a hazelnut, lying in the palm of my hand, and I perceived that it was as round as any ball. I looked at it and thought: What can this be? And I was given this general answer: It is everything that is made. I was amazed that it could last for I thought it was so little that it could suddenly fall into nothing.

"And I was answered in my understanding: It lasts and always will, because God loves it; and thus everything has being through the love of God. In this little thing I saw three things: The first is that God made it, the second is that he loves it, the third is that God preserves it. But what is that to me? It is that God is the Creator and the lover and protector."

87. When the body's racked with pain

7.7.7.5　　　　　　　　Suggested tune: CA' THE YOWES TAE THE KNOWES

1. When the body's racked with pain,
treatments all applied in vain,
dare to think a cure remains:
God's love can heal us.

2. When the spirit's crushed or torn,
when no joy comes with the dawn,
seek the gift of hope reborn:
God's love can heal us.

3. When the flower of friendship dies,
through suspicion, fear or lies,
hear the voice that calms our cries:
God's love can heal us.

4. When the nations come to blows,
turning friends to murd'rous foes,
even faced with such great woes,
God's love can heal us.

5. When our course is nearly run,
when the thread of life is spun,
fear not what's been left undone.
God's love will heal us.

Stephen Linstead

Words © Copyright 2016 Stainer & Bell Ltd. Reprinted by permission.

Stephen Linstead was a regular participant in our writers' weekends, and this text was written at the 2015 weekend at the Windermere Centre. The theme was healing, and the editorial notes that "Stephen has chosen to set the text to traditional tune CA' THE YOWES TAE THE KNOWES. This is an interesting and brilliant choice as the dramatic 'scotch snaps' which occur throughout the tune bring to mind sharp intakes of breaths as the sufferer moves."

We were joined at the weekend by editors of the forthcoming (at the time) collection, *Hymns of Hope and Healing* (2017), and a number of the hymns written at the weekend found a place in that book. Stephen's moving exploration of healing is one of these.

88. When the church of Jesus

Carlton R. Young

SUTTON

6.5.6.5.D

1. When the church of Jesus
shuts its outer door,
lest the roar of traffic
drown the voice of prayer:
may our prayers, Lord, make us
ten times more aware
that the world we banish
is our Christian care.

2. If our hearts are lifted
where devotion soars
high above this hungry,
suffering world of ours:
lest our hymns should drug us
to forget its needs,
forge our Christian worship
into Christian deeds.

3. Lest the gifts we offer,
money, talents, time,
serve to salve our conscience
to our secret shame:
Lord, reprove, inspire us
by the way you give;
teach us, dying Saviour,
how true Christians live.

Fred Pratt Green
Words © Copyright 1969 and Music © Copyright 2001
Stainer & Bell Ltd. Reprinted by permission.

Fred Pratt Green is one of the best-known hymn writers of the twentieth century, and a prime mover in the Hymn Explosion of the 1960s and 1970s. Amazingly, for those who were there, news of his death came during a conference, *Singing the New Millennium* (see Preface), funded in part by the Pratt Green Trust, established from the proceeds of his own writing, to encourage and support hymn singing and writing, and still active in that cause.

This hymn was published in one of the first hymn supplements, which were the bridge over which radical new material made its way into the next generations of denominational hymnbooks. These hymns turned the Church outwards, to the realities of the world which it so signally often failed to reach.

The tune printed here was among the high points of the memorial commemorations honouring Fred Pratt Green held on 9 June 2001 at Wesley's Chapel, London. It is part of a fine anthem setting of his much-loved hymn, commissioned from the leading American composer Carlton R. Young, based on his tune SUTTON, which, with its distinctive melody and bold harmonies, offers a fresh and excitingly modern new accompaniment to this popular text. The anthem setting is available from Stainer & Bell Ltd (Ref. W205).

89. Who knows now?

Enshrined
Who knows now
what happened on the Emmaus road,
why Ruth should glean amid the alien corn
or why a man should die upon a cross?

Yet all these stories, this once-held belief,
denial of which impoverishes our world,
are set as if in amber, are enshrined
forever in the literature of our land,
and each new generation must tease out
the hidden meanings which, in years gone by,
were common currency for rich or poor,
the highly-educated and the humble serf.

There will be those who find the jewel enshrined
and are inspired to go back to the source,
and some will find there literature for life,
an authorized version of the way to live.

Pam Gidney

Over the years, we have included a number of Pam Gidney's poems and hymns in *Worship Live.* This poem appeared in an issue focused on Connectedness including connections between scripture and life. What happens when the old knowledge of the Bible, which was once seemingly enshrined in our common life, slips into oblivion? The jewel is still there but must be sought out by new generations.

90. Why stand gazing?

Ascension

4.3.7.7.7	Suggested tune: UNIVERSITY COLLEGE

1. Why stand gazing?
What's to see?
Christ, who came to set us free,
now demands we turn around,
tell the world where love is found.

2. Why stand gazing?
Look and act!
Show to all salvation's fact.
Christ, by highest heaven adored,
brings new life to be explored.

3. Why stand gazing?
Wasting time!
Show our Master is divine.
Act, that by our words and deeds,
we may go where Jesus leads.

Alan Camp

In an issue of *Worship Live* on Enjoying Life here is a hymn for Ascension Day, which uses the words of the angel in Acts 1:11 to turn the worshipper round, no longer to gaze after the departed Jesus, but instead to face the world with the message and power of Christ. The sense of urgency of action is true to the author of the text. Alan Camp was a congregational minister and a great encourager of others. Why stand gazing, indeed, when there is "new life to be explored"!

91. Worlds of wonders teeming round us

8.7.8.7.D

1. Worlds of wonders teeming round us,
spring to being at God's voice;
word of God, made flesh among us,
seen in every sufferer's eyes;
deep within, creative spirit,
quickening gifts of sight and sound—
these are all God's presence, secret
till the Bible makes him known.

2. In its words are firm foundation
for a life lived out in trust,
grounded in the resurrection
that brought hope when all was lost:
making ever new the story
that began in ancient songs,
promising the final glory
for which all creation longs.

3. Through its words we shape our living,
learn the weight of God's command;
hearing still the prophets' preaching—
mercy, justice his demand;
then its final revelation,
through the Word come from above,
that the way of our salvation,
and the final word, is love.

Alan Luff

Words © 1999 Stainer & Bell Ltd. Reprinted by permission.

Alan Luff was one of the figures at the heart of the Hymn Explosion of the 1960s and 1970s. He was present at the music consultation at Dunblane in 1963, and his hymns appeared in hymn supplements and the denominational books that followed, including recently, *Rejoice and Sing* (1991) and *Singing the Faith* (2011). He was deeply involved in the Hymn Society of Great Britain and Ireland, and we were honoured that he was also a supporter of *Worship Live*. His hymns are thoughtful and biblical. This hymn appeared in an issue focused on the Word of God, in creation, in prophecy and incarnate in the living Word.

It attracted two new tunes, which appeared in a later issue: SPROWSTON ST CUTHBERT by Basil Bridge, which is printed with it here; and CREATIVE SPIRIT by Marlene Phillips, long-time member of the editorial committee. Marlene writes:

Basil Bridge's tune is full of certainty. It is strong and definite. There is no doubting here. G major is firmly established and even when the mood darkens momentarily with an unexpected move to C major (and with a nod towards A minor at "deep within, creative spirit") it is back in G major again by the end of that section... Basil Bridge travels in a sunny climate.

Although I, too, return to a firm cadence at the end of each phrase of my tune, and have the usual high note a few chords into the last section, it has a different feel. At "word of God" there is a chord of B flat minor, followed by F minor and G minor chords, eventually modulating to D minor and A minor... their presence contributes to the more mysterious and questioning landscape.

Conclusion

I started my active involvement with *Worship Live* at the 2011 conference of the Hymn Society. I had been a subscriber to *Worship Live* for a couple of years and was very much impressed by the breadth and variety of resources in the magazine.

I was delighted when Janet Wootton invited me to join the editorial committee. At that time, the group met at the home of Marlene Phillips in the Lake District. I found it an interesting process as we worked our way through many lever-arch files to find suitable and relevant material. It was intense and exciting work as each issue emerged through our discussions.

It was around this time that the original publisher, Stainer & Bell, felt that they could no longer continue to support the publication. After much discussion the committee decided to try establishing *Worship Live* as an online publication. We were very keen to keep the community vibrant and to this end continued to plan weekend writing workshops. By this time, I was joint editor of *Worship Live* with Janet Wootton. I set up a basic website and organized these hymn writing weekends.

Although I'm not a hymn writer myself, I joined in fully with the writing and exploring process. How wonderful, on the Sunday morning, to put together a full service with many new hymns and prayers. I organized three such weekends, and it was at the last of these, in Suffolk, that the idea of putting together a "Best of Worship Live" collection was first mooted.

Initially we had high hopes for an online magazine, but it soon became apparent that the virtual environment was not a good fit for *Worship Live*. After a total of 64 issues, we decided to cease publication. Even so, we were very much aware that this rich treasury should not become inaccessible to the worshipping community.

At the end of summer 2021, I met Janet in London to discuss the possibility of producing a volume with the working title "The Best of Worship Live".

This volume is the result of many hours' reacquainting ourselves with the many gems in each magazine. It has been an interesting, exciting and humbling process as every edition received scrupulous attention so that nothing should be lost. Of course, difficult decisions about what to include have been made and we had to decide very early on only to include one item from any given contributor. Even so, we feel that this volume represents the marvellous work of a vibrant hymn writing community.

The publication of this printed volume marks the end of our joint collaboration. However, we have noted in our studies of *Worship Live* that there is a rich trove still to be explored. Therefore we plan to make all the editions of *Worship Live* available on a dedicated website for worship leaders and planners. There will be more information in due course on this book's website: https://www.sacristy.co.uk/book/worship-live.

We offer this collection, *First Flight Feathers: The Best of Worship Live,* to our contributors and thank them all for their involvement in *Worship Live.*

Gillian Warson
January 2023

Bibliography

A New Zealand Prayer Book | He Karakia Mihinare o Aotearoa, <https://anglicanprayerbook.nz/054.html>, accessed 28 January 2023.

Alleluia Aotearoa (1993), Palmerston North, NZ: The New Zealand Hymnbook Trust Inc.

Arthurton, M. (1995), "At the Ceasefire", from *Fragments of War and Peace,* Bosnian Arts Project.

Berry, J., Pratt A. et al. (eds) (2017), *Hymns of Hope and Healing: words and music to refresh the Church's ministry of healing*, London: Stainer & Bell.

Boyce-Tillman, J. and Braley, B. (1974), *New Horizons: Songs and hymns for younger children*, London: Galliard.

Boyce-Tillman, J. and Wootton, J. (eds) (1993), *Reflecting Praise*, London: Stainer & Bell and Women in Theology.

Braley, B. and Luff, A. (eds) (1988–), *Hymns and Congregational Songs: A periodical publication of new material,* London: Stainer & Bell.

Burling, D., <https://sermonsinsong.wordpress.com/>, accessed 23 January 2023.

Church Hymnary (fourth edition) (2005), Norwich: Canterbury Press.

Dobson, M. (2019), *Unravelling the Mysteries: Drama, hymns, prayers and poems exploring faith and doubt*, London: Stainer & Bell.

Downing, E. S. (2011), *For Us, God's People Now*, The Leupold Foundation.

Ferguson, C. (2018), *Dare to Believe*, Hastings: Print2Demand.

Fraser, I. and Rennie, D. (1995), *Try-It-Out Hymnbook*, Private Publication, Iona Community.

Gaunt, A. (2003), *Delight that Never Dies: Hymn Texts 1997–2003,* London: Stainer & Bell Hymnquest.

<https://www.stainer.co.uk/hymnquest/>, accessed 30 January 2023.

Jarvis, J. (ed.) (1995), *Big Blue Planet: and other songs for worship in God's world: for young children to share with everyone*, London: Stainer & Bell and the Methodist Church Division of Education and Youth.

Murray, S. (1992), *In Every Corner Sing*, Carol Stream, IL: Hope Publishing Company.

Pratt Green, F., Braley, B. et al. (eds) (1979), *Partners in Praise*, London: Stainer & Bell and the Methodist Church Division of Education and Youth.

Pratt, A. (1999), *Sound Bytes: 94 songs for the 21st Century for children to share with everyone*, London: Stainer & Bell.

Pratt, A. and Dobson, M. (2006), *Poppies and Snowdrops: Resources for times of grief and bereavement*, Peterborough: Inspire.

Rejoice and Sing (1991), Oxford: Published by Oxford University Press for the United Reformed Church.

Sharrocks, P. (2010), *Roots and Wings: Songs of hope in a troubled world*, London: Stainer & Bell.

Singing the Faith (2011), London: Published on behalf of the Trustees for Methodist Church Purposes by Hymns Ancient & Modern.

Skinner, R. (1988), *Leaping and Staggering*, Exeter: Dilettante.

Skinner, R. (2017), *Colliding With God: New and selected poems of faith and doubt*, Glasgow: Wild Goose Publications.

Smith, P. and Boyce-Tillman, J. (eds) (1972), *New Orbit: Songs and hymns for under elevens*, London: Galliard.

Smith, P. (ed.) (1967), *Faith, Folk and Clarity: A collection of folk songs*, Great Yarmouth: Galliard.

Smith, P. (ed.) (1968), *Faith, Folk and Nativity: A new collection of songs*, Great Yarmouth: Galliard.

Smith, P. (ed.) (1969), *Faith, Folk and Festivity: A collection of songs*, Great Yarmouth: Galliard.

Story Song (1993), London: Stainer & Bell and Methodist Church Division of Education and Youth.

UK Song Writing Contest <https://www.songwritingcontest.co.uk/>, accessed 23 January 2023.

Warson, G. (2006), *Healing the Nations: Fred Kaan, the man and his hymns*, London: Stainer & Bell.

Warson, G. (2021), *Enjoying Vintage Hymns in Worship: Hidden treasures rediscovered for today's church*, Durham: Sacristy Press.

Wetmore, H., <https://gatewaynews.co.za/singing-the-word-to-one-another-hugh-wetmore/>, accessed 23 January 2023.

Wootton, J. (2007), *Eagles' Wings and Lesser Things*, London: Stainer & Bell.

Wootton, J. (2010), *This is our Song: Women's Hymnwriting*, London: Epworth Press.

Copyright Acknowledgments

The editors are grateful to all those who have given permission for copyright material to be included. Every effort has been made to trace and contact copyright owners and controllers, and apologies are extended to anyone whose rights have inadvertently not been acknowledged. Any omissions or inaccuracies of copyright detail, brought to the attention of the editors, will be corrected in subsequent printings.

Applications for the use of material with individual copyrights may be made via contact details on this book's website (see page iii). Where applicable, and where the user holds a valid licence, some copyright material may be used through the CCLI Licensing Scheme: <https://uk.ccli.com>.

1. © Sue Wade and Latimer Congregational Church, Stepney (Thursday Fellowship). Reprinted by permission.
2. Music © Copyright 2007 Stainer & Bell Ltd, 23 Gruneisen Road, London N3 1LS, www.stainer.co.uk. Reprinted by permission.
3. © Ruth Templeman and Kathryn Schofield. Reprinted by permission.
4. © Hazel Hudson. Reprinted by permission.
5. © Graham Adams. Reprinted by permission.
6. © Jenny Spouge. Reprinted by permission.
7. © Carolyn Sanderson. Reprinted by permission.
8. © Copyright 2006 Stainer & Bell Ltd, 23 Gruneisen Road, London N3 1LS, www.stainer.co.uk. Reprinted by permission.
9. © Copyright 2000 Stainer & Bell Ltd, 23 Gruneisen Road, London N3 1LS, www.stainer.co.uk, Music © Dr J. P. Dobbs. Permission sought.
10. © 1994 Janet Lancefield. Reprinted by permission.

11. © Jan Sutch Pickard. Reprinted by permission.
12. Words and Music © 2004 Christopher Humphries. Reprinted by permission.
13. © Frances Ballantyne. Reprinted by permission.
14. Words © Albert Jewell, Music © Sylvia Crowther. Reprinted by permission.
15. © Richard Skinner. Reprinted by permission.
16. © Anne J. Sardeson. Reprinted by permission.
17. © Raymond Vincent. Permission sought.
18. © The Revd John R. Bradley. Permission sought.
19. © Copyright 2004 Stainer & Bell Ltd, 23 Gruneisen Road, London N3 1LS, www.stainer.co.uk. Reprinted by permission.
20. Words and Music © Copyright 1997 Stainer & Bell Ltd, 23 Gruneisen Road, London N3 1LS, www.stainer.co.uk. Reprinted by permission.
21. Music © Tim Barton, Words © Heather Phillips. Permission sought.
22. Words © Copyright 1993, Music © Copyright 1995 Stainer & Bell Ltd, 23 Gruneisen Road, London N3 1LS, www.stainer.co.uk. Reprinted by permission.
23. © 1996 Margot Arthurton. Reprinted by permission.
24. © Margaret Walker. Reprinted by permission.
25. © 2014 Roger Tabor. Reprinted by permission.
26. Words and Music © Louise Counsell. Reprinted by permission.
27. © Maggie Norton. Reprinted by permission.
28. © 2003 Hugh G. Wetmore. Reprinted by permission.
29. © John Coutts. Reprinted by permission.
30. Words © Colin Ferguson, Music © Andrew Lane. Reprinted by permission.
31. © 1992 Hope Publishing Company, www.hopepublishing.com. All rights reserved. Used by permission.
32. © David Mowbray/Jubilate Hymns. Administered by The Jubilate Group, Kitley House, St Katherines Road, Torquay TQ1 4DE, copyrightmanager@jubilate.co.uk. Used by permission.
33. © Copyright 1997 Stainer & Bell Ltd, 23 Gruneisen Road, London N3 1LS, www.stainer.co.uk. Reprinted by permission.

34. Words and Music © Ruth Buckley. Reprinted by permission.
35. © John Lansley. Reprinted by permission.
36. Words © 2010 Kevin Mayhew Ltd, Buxhall, Stowmarket, Suffolk, IP14 3BW. Used by permission. Music © David Lee. Reprinted by permission.
37. © Janet Pybon. Permission sought.
38. © Janet Lees. Reprinted by permission.
39. Music © Carole Elphick. Reprinted by permission.
40. Words © The Estate of Lilian Butler, Music © Peter Sharrocks. Reprinted by permission.
41. © Hilary Jackson. Permission sought.
42. © Revd K. C. Fabricius. Permission sought.
43. Words © Jean Silvan Evans, Music © John Piggins. Reprinted by permission.
44. © 1979 Stainer & Bell Ltd and The Trustees for Methodist Church Purposes (UK), 23 Gruneisen Road, London N3 1LS, www.stainer.co.uk.
45. Words and Music © Basil Bridge. Reprinted by permission.
46. Words and Music © Simon Baynes. Reprinted by permission.
47. © Mary G. Elms. Reprinted by permission.
48. © Carolyn Sanderson. Reprinted by permission.
49. © Stuart J. Brock. Reprinted by permission.
50. © Judi Marsh. Permission sought.
51. © Janet Evans. Reprinted by permission.
52. Words and Music © Copyright 1990 Stainer & Bell Ltd, 23 Gruneisen Road, London N3 1LS, www.stainer.co.uk. Reprinted by permission.
53. © Janice Anstey. Permission sought.
54. © Heather Johnston. Permission sought.
55. © Sheila Baldock. Permission sought.
56. Words © Copyright 1997 Stainer & Bell Ltd, 23 Gruneisen Road, London N3 1LS, www.stainer.co.uk; Music © Jenny Canham. Reprinted by permission.
57. © Emma Turl (Admin by ChurchSongs.co.uk). Reprinted by permission.

58. Words and Music © Maggie Hamilton. Reprinted by permission.
59. © Wendy White. Reprinted by permission.
60. © Christopher Idle. Reprinted by permission.
61. Words © Jenny Wakely/Jubilate Hymns. Administered by The Jubilate Group, Kitley House, St Katherines Road, Torquay TQ1 4DE, copyrightmanager@jubilate.co.uk. Used by permission; Music © Gill Gilbert. Reprinted by permission.
62. Words and Music © Copyright 2003 Stainer & Bell Ltd, 23 Gruneisen Road, London N3 1LS, www.stainer.co.uk. Reprinted by permission.
63. Words and Music © Jeanne Blowers. Permission sought.
64. Words and Music © Copyright 2006 Stainer & Bell Ltd, 23 Gruneisen Road, London N3 1LS, www.stainer.co.uk. Reprinted by permission.
65. © Carol Dixon. Reprinted by permission.
66. © Copyright 2000 Stainer & Bell Ltd, 23 Gruneisen Road, London N3 1LS, www.stainer.co.uk.
67. © John Adamson Brown. Permission sought.
68. © Dominic Grant. Reprinted by permission.
69. © Kaye Lee. Reprinted by permission.
70. © Hugh Naunton. Reprinted by permission.
71. © Patricia Randall. Reprinted by permission.
72. © Wayne Leupold Editions Inc. The Leupold Foundation, 8510 Triad Drive, Colfax, NC 27235, USA. contact@theleupoldfoundation.org. www.theleupoldfoundation.org. Reprinted by permission.
73. © Tom Wilkinson. Reprinted by permission.
74. Words © Moira Rose. Arrangement © Copyright 2000 Stainer & Bell Ltd, 23 Gruneisen Road, London N3 1LS, www.stainer.co.uk. Reprinted by permission.
75. Words and Music © Sue Gilmurray. Reprinted by permission.
76. © Chris Guest and the Year 5 pupils of The Paragon School, Bath. Permission sought.
77. Words © Neville Ashton, Music © Neville Favell. Reprinted by permission.
78. © John Helliwell. Permission sought.

79. © Sara Iles. Reprinted by permission.
80. © Jan Grimwood. Reprinted by permission.
81. © David Lemmon. Permission sought.
82. Words and Music © Copyright 1993 Stainer & Bell Ltd, 23 Gruneisen Road, London N3 1LS, www.stainer.co.uk. Reprinted by permission.
83. Words © Sheila Kelly and pupils of Yealand Primary School, Music © Marlene Phillips. Reprinted by permission.
84. © Copyright 2007 Stainer & Bell Ltd, 23 Gruneisen Road, London N3 1LS, www.stainer.co.uk. Reprinted by permission.
85. Copyright 2001 © Gareth Hill Publishing/Song Solutions CopyCare, 14 Horsted Square, Uckfield, TN22 1QG www.songsolutions.org. Reprinted by permission.
86. Words © Norman Goreham, Music © Bill Chessum. Reprinted by permission.
87. © Copyright 2016 Stainer & Bell Ltd, 23 Gruneisen Road, London N3 1LS, www.stainer.co.uk. Reprinted by permission.
88. Words © Copyright 1969 and Music © Copyright 2001 Stainer & Bell Ltd, 23 Gruneisen Road, London N3 1LS, www.stainer.co.uk. Reprinted by permission.
89. © Pam Gidney. Permission sought.
90. © The Executrix for Valerie E. Camp. Permission sought.
91. © Copyright 1999 Stainer & Bell Ltd, 23 Gruneisen Road, London N3 1LS, www.stainer.co.uk; Music © Basil Bridge. Reprinted by permission.

Index of Composers

Composers of tunes printed in the book

Ainger, Lois	82
Barton, Tim	21
Baynes, Simon	46
Blowers, Jeanne	63
Boyce-Tillman, June	64
Bridge, Basil E.	45, 91
Buckley, Ruth	34
Canham, Jenny	56
Chessum, Bill	86
Counsell, Louise	26
Crowther, Sylvia	14
Danks, Nicholas	2
Dobbs, Jack	9
Elphick, Carole	39
Favell, Neville	77
Gilbert, Gill	61
Gilmurray, Sue	75
Hamilton, Maggie	58
Haywood, Alan	52
Humphries, Christopher	12
Lancefield, Janet	10
Lane, Andrew	30
Lee, David	36
Mews, Douglas	31
Phillips, Marlene	22, 83
Piggins, John	43

Sharp, Ian 62
Sharrocks, Peter 40
Thomas, Ruthie 20
Young, Carlton 88

Index of Tunes

This includes new tunes printed in the book, and new/existing tunes recommended by name but not included.
* = tune printed in the book

ABBOTS LEIGH 25	ELLERS 7
ALDWICK GRANGE* 62	FOURTH WATCH* 45
ALL FOR JESUS 53	GENTLE* 26
ALL THINGS BRIGHT AND BEAUTIFUL 1	GOD OF MY ALL* 30
AND I HAVE CALLED YOU BY NAME* 2	HAZELNUT* 86
	HEART OF GOD* 22
AR HYD Y NOS 68	HOLY SPIRIT HOVERING, BROODING* 34
ASHGROVE 40	HOLY WELL* 74
AUSTRIA 28	HONOR THE EARTH* 31
AVON MEADOWS* 77	HOSANNA* 14
BLAENWERN 25	IN EXILE* 82
CAMBRIDGE 21	KINGSLEY* 61
CARRY ME SHEPHERD* 52	LADYWELL 33
CA'T HE YOWES TAE THE KNOWES 87	LONDON 16
	LUX EOI 8
CHRISTMAS LIGHTS* 10	MANY TEARS: ONE SORROW* 39
CRADLE SONG 5	MARCHING 48
CRYING FOR THE WORLD* .. 20	MERLE'S TUNE 72
DA ISLES OF GLETNESS 73	MIT FREUDEN ZART 80
DANIEL 49	NOEL NOUVELET 24
DISADVANTAGE* 75	O JESULEIN SÜSS 18
DIVINITY* 21	OH MY SPIRIT* 63
EAST ACKLAM 68	OWLACOMBE* 9

187

PO KARE KARE 84	STAFFA* 12
REDBANK* 43	SUTTON* 88
SACRED SONGS AND SOLOS	THE BARD OF ARMAGH 42
405 17	UNIVERSITY COLLEGE 90
SERVANT SONG 79	VOX DILECTI 85
SHOUT JUBILEE* 58	WINCHESTER NEW 81
SING OUR SONGS* 36	WINDRUSH* 56
SONG 1 19	WINKFIELD* 46
SONG OF THE SUN* 64	WONDERING* 40
SPROWSTON ST CUTHBERT* 91	YEALAND HARVEST SONG* . . 83
ST HELEN 70	

Index of Authors

Adams, Graham 5
Adamson Brown, John 67
Ainger, Lois 82
Anstey, Janice 53
Arthurton, Margot 23
Ashton, Neville 77
Baldock, Sheila 55
Ballantyne, Frances 13
Baynes, Simon 46
Blowers, Jeanne 63
Boyce-Tillman, June 64
Bradley, John 18
Braley, Bernard 44
Bridge, Basil E. 45
Brock, Stuart J. 49
Buckley, Ruth 34
Butler, Lilian 40
Camp, Alan 90
Cosnett, Elizabeth 62
Counsell, Louise 26
Coutts, John 29
Dixon, Carol 65
Dobson, Marjorie 8
Elms, Mary 47
Evans, Janet 51
Fabricius, Kim 42
Ferguson, Colin 30
Fraser, Ian 22

Gaunt, Alan 66
Gidney, Pam 89
Gilmurray, Sue 75
Goreham, Norman 86
Grant, Dominic 68
Grimwood, Jan 80
Guest, Chris 76
Hamilton, Maggie 58
Helliwell, John 78
Hill, Gareth 85
Horner, Alan 3
Hudson, Hazel 4
Humphries, Christopher 12
Idle, Christopher 60
Iles, Sara 79
Jackson, Hilary 41
Jewell, Albert 14
Johnston, Heather 54
Kelly, Sheila 83
Lancefield, Janet 10
Lansley, John 35
Leckebusch, Martin E. 36
Lee, Kaye 69
Leech, Oliver 9
Lees, Janet 38
Lemmon, David 81
Linstead, Stephen 87
Luff, Alan 91

Marsh, Judi 50	Skinner, Richard 15
Mowbray, David 32	Spouge, Jenny 6
Murray, Shirley Erena 31	Sutch Pickard, Jan 11
Naunton, Hugh 70	Tabor, Roger 25
Norton, Maggie 27	Taylor, Cecily 52
Paragon School, Bath 76	Thomas, Bill 19
Phillips, Heather 21	Thomas, Ruthie 20
Pratt, Andrew 56	Turl, Emma 57
Pratt Green, Fred 88	Vincent, Raymond 17
Pybon, Janet 37	Wade, Sue 1
Randall, Patricia 71	Wakely, Jenny 61
Rose, Moira 74	Walker, Margaret 24
Sanderson, Carolyn 7	Wetmore, Hugh G 28
Sanderson, Mike 48	White, Wendy 59
Sardeson, Anne J 16	Wilkinson, Tom 73
Silvan Evans, Jean 43	Wootton, Janet 84
Sinclair Downing, Edith 72	Wright, Ambrose D 33

Index of First lines and titles

Titles are in italics.

*A Hymn in Acknowledgment of
    Prayer*.......................... 77
*A morning prayer giving thanks for
    the night*...................... 54
A Resurrection Hymn............ 46
Accident 15
Advice 69
All our days 49
All things good and medical 1
Amnesty 32
And I have called you by name.... 2
And I saw Jesus 43
And the elder brother 3
Article............................4
Ascension 90
At the Well 71
Away in a Manger (revisited)...... 5
Away in a manger we choose to find
    Christ....................... 5
Bless the Lord all created things... 6
Bright Sunday's waving palms are
    fading fast 7
By a monument of marble 8
By grace bestowed, so undeserved. 9
By the light of a flickering lantern 10
Caedmon...................... 11

Can you trace the pattern of the rays
    of the sun?................... 12
Carry me Shepherd 52
Choosing to return home........ 13
Christmas Lights 10
Clap your hands all you trees! ... 14
Colliding with God 15
Come dare to live in the world
    today 16
Come, for everything's ready, all the
    tables are laid............... 17
Come in to the warmth.......... 18
Come, vast eternal dance of one-in-
    three....................... 19
Communion-in-Trinity 19
Conversion...................... 3
*Creed of a Speech and Language
    Therapist*................... 38
Crying for the world 20
Deep in the core of earth 21
Deep in the heart of God 22
Disadvantage 75
Don't forget your lunch box 23
Early Easter morning—all were sunk
    in fear...................... 24
Enshrined....................... 89

Expectation—A meditation 65
For a retirement 29
For the Healing of Nations 63
Founder of the laws of motion ... 25
Gentle to understand 26
Go canny Brother Aidan! Iona's rocks are sharp 27
God became a man in Jesus...... 28
God in Jesus..................... 28
God of love and grace........... 29
God of my all.................... 30
God of my faith, I offer you my doubt 30
God of the galaxies spinning in space 31
Great is God's truth, it shall prevail 32
Great Orme, Advent Sunday 35
Hazelnut....................... 86
Healing the Church.............. 81
Held captive by the king of love .. 33
Holy Spirit hovering, brooding... 34
Hopkins, your bright kestrel 35
Hosanna....................... 14
How are we to sing our songs to you? 36
How did it come to this?......... 37
Hymn for Eastertide............. 24
Hymn for the New Year.......... 25
I believe in God, Creator, Image maker..................... 38
I wish that my eyes were fountains of tears..................... 39
I wonder, might Joseph.......... 40

I wouldn't touch him with a bargepole 41
Imagine a World................ 42
Imagine a world where our leaders aren't liars................... 42
In a land that was parched and baked dry by sun............. 43
In affairs of economics 44
In Exile 82
In the dark before the dawn...... 45
In the silence of the midnight 46
In the stillness of this moment ... 47
Isles of the North Rejoice.......... 73
Journeying on a day of darkness.. 48
Judas.......................... 37
Knowing us from eternity 49
Lady in the Shadows............. 50
Landfall with Columba, AD 563... 27
Let justice roll like waters........ 51
Lift me up on your shoulder, Shepherd.................... 52
Listen! Mary tells the story 53
Lord God, we thank you 54
Lord Jesus, help us stand 55
Love soars where eagles cease to fly 56
Many Tears: One Sorrow 39
Metaprayer 47
Millions of migrants, on the run . 57
Must we starve our children to pay our debts?................... 58
My God is beyond all imagining . 59
My mother—she was lovely!..... 60
No height so high, no depth so low 61

O God, by whom our yesterdays . 62
O sun of Wisdom, arise 64
Oh my Spirit will flow like the river
    of life 63
Oh the bliss of a bit of shelter 65
On Calvary, life's light........... 66
Our wonder grows and deepens
    with the years................ 67
Out of the mouths of babes:
    Bathsheba's little boy.......... 60
Present at the world's creation ... 68
Ruth, don't do it. 69
Schoolday...................... 23
See he comes in modest manner . 70
She is the tree of life.............. 79
She threw the bucket down the
    well....................... 71
Shout Jubilee 58
Sing praise for Hebrew midwives. 72
Soaked by the spray from these
    turbulent waters 73
Song of the Sun.................. 64
The Cup 9
The gift of Caedmon............. 11
The holiness of God is veiled 74
The Prodigal Returns............ 13
The Rays of the Sun 12

The soldiers by and large were
    decent men.................. 75
These are the hands 76
These are the hands that have done
    so much harm 76
To pray is to extol................ 77
Tread Softly in the Close.......... 78
Tread softly 78
Tree of wisdom, give us shelter... 79
We celebrate God's word to us ... 80
We happily could spend our days. 81
We know the songs of Zion from our
    youth 82
We love....................... 83
Weep with us for the islands 84
When mountains that we thought
    secure...................... 85
When seen from vastnesses of
    space 86
When the body's racked with pain 87
When the church of Jesus........ 88
Who knows now? 89
Why stand gazing?.............. 90
Wondering 40
Worlds of wonders teeming round
    us 91
Yealand Harvest Song 83

Index of Bible texts

Genesis 1 91	Isaiah 2:4 85
Genesis 1:1–2 68	Isaiah 40:26 31
Genesis 1:2 34	Isaiah 40:31 74
Genesis 1:14–19 . . . . 25, 31	Isaiah 43:1 2
Genesis 1:26–7 . . . . 38, 81	Isaiah 49:16 74
Genesis 2:7 . . . . 19, 59	Isaiah 53:4 60
Genesis 2:8,15 31	Isaiah 54:10 85
Genesis 4:9 16	Isaiah 55:12 14
Genesis 11:1–9 68	Isaiah 61:1 68
Exodus 1:15-22 72	Jeremiah 1:5 49
Exodus 2:1–10 72	Jeremiah 9:1 39
Leviticus 25 58	Jeremiah 18:1–6 19
Deuteronomy 32:11 49	Amos 4:1 44
Ruth 1:15–17 69	Amos 5:21–4 44
Ruth 2:1–17 89	Amos 5:24 51
2 Samuel 11—12 60	Amos 8:4–6 44
Job 50	Zechariah 9:9 37
Job 38:31–3 31	Matthew 1:1,6 60
Psalm 23:5 9	Matthew 2:1–11 10
Psalm 46:1 85	Matthew 4:1–11 28
Psalm 51 60	Matthew 4:18–22 29
Psalm 114 57	Matthew 8:14–15 41
Psalm 137:1–6 82	Matthew 10:29–30 60
Psalm 137:4 36	Matthew 21, 22 28
Psalm 139:15–16 49	Matthew 21:8–11 . . . . 7, 37, 70
Proverbs 3:18 79	Matthew 21:12 . . . . 7, 37, 70
Proverbs 8:22–3; 27–8 59	Matthew 22:1–14 17
Proverbs 9:3 38	Matthew 22:20–22 37

Matthew 25:21 29	Luke 4:38–39..................... 41
Matthew 25:40 43	Luke 14:15–24 .... 17, 19
Matthew 26:15 37	Luke 15:4–7...................... 52
Matthew 26:37–42............... 70	Luke 15:11–32 .... 3, 13
Matthew 26:40–3.................. 7	Luke 19:37–40 ....7, 14, 70
Matthew 26:55 75	Luke 19:45................7, 37, 70
Matthew 26:69–74................ 7	Luke 20:25 37
Matthew 27:11–31............... 75	Luke 22:2,5 28
Matthew 27:22–3.................. 7	Luke 22:3 28
Matthew 27:45–50,65,66 28	Luke 22:6 28
Matthew 27:45–54................ 7	Luke 22:41–4..................... 70
Matthew 28:2 46	Luke 22:45–6...................... 7
Matthew 28:8 53	Luke 22:52–3..................... 75
Matthew 28:19–20............... 68	Luke 22:56–62 7
Mark 1:29–34 28	Luke 22:63–7..................... 75
Mark 1:30–31 41	Luke 23:1–25..................... 75
Mark 9:24 30	Luke 23:21–5...................... 7
Mark 11:8–10 .... 7, 70	Luke 23:44–9...................... 7
Mark 11:15–17 ....7, 37, 70	Luke 24:1–12..................... 53
Mark 12:17 37	Luke 24:2........................ 46
Mark 14:32–38 70	Luke 24:13–35 ....46, 48, 89
Mark 14:37–40 7	Luke 24:30–5..................... 53
Mark 14:48–9 75	John 1:10 28
Mark 14:66–72 7	John 1:14 ....28, 80, 91
Mark 15 75	John 2:13–16..............7, 37, 70
Mark 15:13–15 7	John 3:8 12
Mark 15:33–9 7	John 3:16 18
Mark 16:1–4 53	John 4:7–15...................... 71
Mark 16:4....................... 46	John 6:66 7
Luke 1:26–38.................28, 65	John 8:36 29
Luke 1:57 65	John 12:12–15................ 7, 70
Luke 2:1–7...................... 65	John 12:31–33................... 28
Luke 2:7 5	John 13:2–17.................... 28
Luke 2:7–20..................... 10	John 15:26 34
Luke 2:22 28	John 16:7–15.................... 34

John 18:19–40	75
John 19:1–16	75
John 19:34	15
John 20:1–7	46, 53
John 20:3–10	24
John 20:11–16	24
John 20:19	46
John 20:24–9	24
John 20:27	15, 19
Acts 1:11	90
Acts 2:4	68
Acts 2:22	28
Acts 2:32,33	28
Acts 4:12	28
Acts 20:29	28
Romans 3:24	9
Romans 8:14–17	34
Romans 8:26–7	34
Romans 8:38–9	61
Romans 12:3–8	73
1 Corinthians 11:25	9
1 Corinthians 11:24	12, 19
1 Corinthians 12:1–31	34, 73
1 Corinthians 12:13	68
1 Corinthians 13:1–13	34
2 Corinthians 5:19	28
Galatians 5:22–3	34
Ephesians 1:19,20	28
Ephesians 4:7–14	19, 73
Ephesians 4:11–12	34, 73
Philippians 2:9–11	68
Hebrews 2:17	28
1 Peter 2:24	60
1 John 1:5–7	81
1 John 4:7–11	81
Revelation 7:3	85
Revelation 7:9–10	68
Revelation 19:16	28
Revelation 22:1–5	63

EU GPSR Authorized Representative:

LOGOS EUROPE, 9 rue Nicolas Poussin, 17000 La Rochelle, France

contact@logoseurope.eu